N 1· 11· C

In memory of my brother Robert Eugene Osing,
whose life was an embodiment of the truth
that Christianity is a way of living, not a way of thinking.

Love at Midlife

Building and Rebuilding Relationships

RICHARD A. OSING

Rudi Publishing
San Francisco

Rudi Publishing, 12 Geary St., Suite 508, San Francisco CA 94108

ISBN 0-945213-31-X

First Edition

PRINTED IN THE UNITED STATES OF AMERICA

Vaughan Printing, Nashville TN

Library of Congress Cataloging-in-Publication Data

Osing, Richard A. (Richard Allen)

    Love at midlife : bulding and rebuilding relationships / Richard A. Osing. -- 1st ed.

      p.   cm.

    Includes bibliographical references (p.   ) and index.

    ISBN 0-945213-31-x (pbk.)

    1. Middle aged persons--United States--Psychology. 2. Middle aged persons--United

States--Family relationships. I. Title.

HQ1059.5.U5084 1998

305.244--dc21   98-20707

                                        CIP

98   99   00   01   02   03   04   05   06   07   10 9 8 7 6 5 4 3 2 1

Kristin K. Boekhoff, Cover Designer

David Featherstone, Editor

Contents

Acknowledgments

I graduated from seminary intending to make my mark on the world as a teacher of the Bible, but soon discovered that I was in demand, not as a teacher, but as a counselor. Many people, in and out of the church, were having painful marriage and family problems. The parish ministry was the context of my counseling for many years. In my more than forty years of working with families and their problems I have also served as a counselor at an alternative high school, as the executive director of a crisis intervention program, as the executive director of an agency providing counseling and support services to the elderly and their families, and as a family and marriage counselor in a psychiatric clinic.

I wrote my first book, *How To Love & Be Loved*, because I was convinced that much of the problem with relationships in America was that people did not know how to love. In the last ten years I have been impressed by the increasing numbers of people requesting counseling after twenty or twenty-five years of marriage. These midlife marriages were showing up more frequently in divorce courts. Yet I could not find material to address this phenomenon. This book is written to begin to fill that gap with the desire that it will be not only helpful, but also hopeful for people in midlife.

A lot of people have encouraged me to complete this project. First and foremost, is my wife, Jo. She has so graciously prodded me and supported me in so many ways through our twenty years of marriage that is is impossible to do justice with a simple acknowledgment. Together, Jo and I have gone through the adjustments of midlife, and my life has been blessed by her love and companionship through so many experiences. My three children, Mark, Matt, and Mary, and my two stepchildren, Steve and Anne Fairchild, have also been very supportive, and I am grateful that, during the writing of this book, daughter Mary and her husband Dan presented us with our first grandchild, Owen Thomas Welch.

Terri Boekhoff, my publisher, makes things easy. She has the patience of Job indeed, but she has been tenacious in her insistence that I still had at least one more book to write. Good friends Ron and Renee Adkins, Barb Iversen, Bob Ferguson, and Larry Eilers have helped by continuing to express their interest in the book in progress. For their much-appreciated assistance in the preparation of the manuscript of this book, I want to thank Jenny Becker, Rick Bowersox, Steve Fairchild, Daniel and Justine Lieurance, Bob Seager, and Deb Thomas. My editor, David Featherstone helped me clarify and articulate my message. I am also grateful to Ginnie Waters and Joshua Bagby who made suggestions that greatly improved the book.

Without the many clients who have trusted me with their stories, however, this book would never have been written. I am grateful to all of them and consider their confidence that I could help them a sacred trust given to me. For that reason I have carefully protected their identities.

Finally, I am grateful to the members of St. Luke's Episcopal Church in Cedar Falls, Iowa, and Christ Episcopal Church in Cedar Rapids, for graciously allowing me the time to invest in the counseling of people with problems without any question of whether they were members of the congregations.

Richard A. Osing
Shrove Tuesday, 1998

Introduction

Alan is a midlife professional, age forty-two. His marriage has been unhappy for at least ten years. He has stayed in the marriage because he believed his career demanded it, and because of the children. He has had two affairs in the past ten years. He has been overwhelmed with guilt about the affairs, but those experiences have also taught him that there is something better that is possible in male/female relationships than what he has experienced in his twenty-two years of marriage. Circumstances beyond his control have brought him to the end of the only career he ever imagined for himself. The future looks bleak. He has a new job—at least he has that much—but it is just that, a job. He seems lost, depressed, and afraid.

He has never thought what it would mean if he were divorced; he has never pictured his life in a way that did not involve the presence of his children. This means that he has almost no pictures to plan the future, only pictures of past life-plans, past expectations. With no template for the future, it is no wonder Alan is in despair and depressed. He is at midlife, but it feels more like the end. It really isn't the end, of course. It is just the beginning of the second half of life. But Alan does not see it that way. Because the plan for his life has not worked out, he can only imagine that he is a failure. He cannot yet imagine the possibility of a new plan—a plan for the next half of his life.

Although Alan feels as though his situation is unique, it is not. Some of the details are, to be sure, but tens of thousands of other men find themselves in similar situations. They, too, started out with their own life-plans and expectations, and somewhere between forty and fifty-five they have also begun to assess where they are in relation to those plans and expectations. Some, see only ruined plans, expectations that have not been fulfilled, and a dead end to their ambitions and careers. A few, in fact, have already realized a large proportion of their ambitions; they have come to the place they wanted to be— mission accomplished. But now they are asking, "Is this all there is?"

Change the scene. We now look at Virginia, a woman in her late forties. She has raised two children, a son and a daughter, and she has endured a marriage of thirty years. Married life was not at all what she expected. She and her husband, John, have had nothing in common since the children left home. In the first five years of the marriage, they had a real economic struggle, and they were partners in that struggle. Both of them had only a high school education; her husband has worked in the same factory for twenty-eight years.

Before the children came, they could not afford to do much; and after the first child, a son, was born, they could afford even less. Most of their socializing was with their parents and with their siblings. Later, she made friends in the neighborhood; he made friends at work. They had no friends in common outside the family.

After eight years of rented apartments, Virginia and John finally made a down payment on a home. Virginia devoted herself to homemaking and parenting and found great fulfillment in that role. She was a devoted mother to the children and developed close relationships with both of them. John was not too involved with the children when they were young. He took an interest in his son during the teenage years and followed his son's high school wrestling activities with great faithfulness. He attended his daughter's softball games, but with slightly less fidelity.

Almost all of Virginia's social life is with her female friends from the neighborhood or church. He does not have a social life, except a few beers with the guys after work. Their only time alone together has been on summer vacation trips to the west, where they look at property on which to build a retirement home.

Six months prior to their thirtieth wedding anniversary, Virginia suddenly makes an appointment with a marriage counselor. She tells the counselor that she has been extremely unhappy for over fifteen years, that her marriage is extremely lonely and not the least bit fulfilling. The counselor is curious as to why she is seeking the counseling now. Why has she not come sooner? Why not later? Her answer: "Because he is retiring in seven months. I have been able to endure it because he has been gone forty to fifty hours per week. But in seven months he will be home all the time; I don't know how I will be able to stand it."

Virginia's situation is precarious financially to say the least. She has had only sporadic part-time employment, which means she has no social security credits of her own. They have some assets, and she will be entitled to some settlement from his pension; but that will not provide much in the way of income. She has decided that she is prepared to get a job. She has taken some business courses at the community college and is preparing, for the first time in her life, to become completely independent.

This is clearly a portrait of a woman at midlife. As she looks back, she sees a fulfilling role of mother and homemaker, but it is not enough to look back on happiness. She wants to see some happiness in the future, too. She realizes that their retirement plans involve a move to a part of the country where they have no friends. It will just be the two of them, at least for a while. He would prefer, in fact, to build that home on some isolated land away from any crowded city or town. The thought of being alone with a man who has almost nothing to say to her feels like being sentenced to solitary confinement. If she has to live alone, she would just as soon really be alone. As she sees it, they have six months to begin to build a viable relationship, or else she will terminate the marriage.

These two stories—and many, many others similar to them—are being repeated today in growing numbers all over America. Just as other problems have increased as the baby boomers have passed through life, midlife problems will increase as well. More and more people who have been married twenty-five years or more are getting divorced. Marriages that have been stable (although not necessarily happy) for enough years to celebrate a silver wedding anniversary are ending up in divorce court.

I believe midlife divorce in the United States is a serious, yet relatively unnoticed crisis. The average person in America believes that divorce is an early-in-the marriage difficulty . . . and it is. Forty percent of all divorces still occur in the first five years of marriage. State legislatures have begun to be concerned because of the damaging effects upon the children whose worlds come apart when their parents divorce. At this writing, at least one dozen states have already acted, or are considering acting, to change the so-called no-fault divorce laws for marriages with children involved. But I find very little concern across the country about the problem of midlife divorce, and yet there should be. Let me quickly list a few reasons why I think midlife divorce is a serious problem.

First, in many cases midlife divorce means that Grandma and Grandpa are getting divorced. In many of the family systems I have worked with in counseling, the grandparents function as anchors. They are the people to whom adult children return for Thanksgiving and Christmas, and they are the most effective spokespersons for family values and identity. What will happen if the family anchors come up and the family begins to drift even faster?

Second, in our contemporary world, divorce at midlife will leave many women more vulnerable to financial stress and economic insecurity. Many women currently reaching midlife do not have an independent economic security. Because it was expected of them, many of these women stayed home, where they were more than adequate homemakers and mothers. But our society still refuses to put a financial value on the contribution that thousands of women make. Similarly, a review of divorce settlements shows that those settlements place no value on women's child-rearing and homemaking activities.

Third, age and education are cruel factors that influence the chances of midlife women to remarry. At least they have been historically. Older men, especially when they are successful and are high wage earners, attract younger women. Almost everybody knows at least one midlife man who has married a woman ten to fifteen years younger than he is. But we don't know many midlife women who can marry a man ten to fifteen years younger. The number of available males, already shrinking as a result of morbidity factors, is thus even lower than it appears since those who have survived tend to look for younger women rather than women their own age.

Fourth, my experience in working with couples and families in the process of divorcing, and in the grieving that follows divorce, persuades me that researcher Judith Wallerstein is correct in *Surviving the Breakup: How Children and Parents Cope with Divorce* when she concludes that, in America, we have underestimated the emotional stress of divorce on adults and children. We have somehow supposed that, since "everybody's doing it," we are all adjusting and divorce is no big deal. It *is* a big deal for adults who are young or old, and for children young or old. I have seen many adult children profoundly distressed by their parents' divorce, and those divorces often have profound effects upon their own marriages or dating relationships.

The purpose of this book, then is to direct a spotlight onto relationships, marriage, divorce, dating, and remarriage at midlife. Much of the material presented here is directed at couples who have been married for several decades. For this I have drawn on my own experience as someone now sixty-five, who at age forty-five became a remarried midlife man. I have also drawn on my experience in counseling many midlife persons going through divorce and remarriage. At the same time, I recognize that a great number of couples in America have similar long-term relationships although they have never gotten married. These people experience the same kinds of relationship pressures at midlife as married couples, and I believe that they can also benefit by reassessing the needs and demands of love and relationships at midlife that I suggest here.

I believe that the causes of midlife marital distress are complex, but that some of the factors can be clearly identified. Further, what holds a marriage together in the first half of life may not hold it together in the second half, and this fact is not widely discussed. The result is that many men and women imagine that what has always kept them together will continue to do so, but midlife divorce is as potentially damaging to America's families as divorce at any other time. Most importantly, I believe that there are steps that married people can take to save their marriages from running out of gas after twenty or thirty years. In addition to the problem of divorce at midlife, there is the problem of starting over with dating and contemplating remarriage at midlife. Starting over when you have been out of the dating scene for twenty or more years is not easy. As the recent car commercial proclaims, "All the rules have changed." Remarriage is not just another marriage, nor is it like a first marriage. Remarriage is something completely different, and all of your previous marital experience will not help you. In fact, some of that experience will hurt you in the adjustment process. This book intends to address those still married at midlife, those divorced or in the process of divorcing at midlife, and those contemplating remarriage at midlife.

The personal names I have just used, as well as the rest of the names in this book, are fictitious. Some of the descriptions and narratives have been changed to protect the confidentiality of clients.

Nevertheless, the situations do represent a truthful picture of the issues, problems, and pains, as well as the joys and happiness, of people at midlife.

Part One

Midlife

Chapter One
The Phenomenon
Called Midlife

People in America are used to the term midlife crisis. We think of it indeed as a crisis that hits one day, and causes a man to leave a promising career or marriage and develop an obsessive craving for a red convertible. He suddenly gets concerned about his paunch and joins an exercise program. Or a woman suddenly announces that she is leaving her marriage and going back to college to get a degree in social work or to take courses so that she can reactivate her teaching certificate. She also signs up for a diet and exercise program to lose twenty pounds.

We tend to think of this kind of behavior as typical of a crisis situation, the implication being that this, too, shall pass. I want to suggest that this is an inappropriate way to think about the midlife phenomenon. It is not a momentary phenomenon that will quickly pass, nor is it something that appears out of the blue. It just looks that way because the person involved has been doing a lot of quiet thinking and reflecting, in a process that has taken months, if not years. It looks like a sudden crisis because it is not until a person begins to take action that anyone else finds out. But it isn't sudden; it is a predictable event in the human life cycle.

A very quiet revolution has been taking place in how we understand the evolution of behavior over a human being's lifetime. One way to characterize that revolution is to say that Jung is in the process of replacing Freud as the psychological guru who best explains life as we are dealing with it. Sigmund Freud's work in psychology has held sway in the western world for over a century. That work, you will remember, suggests that the issues of childhood, especially childhood sexual development, remain the issues we will deal with throughout all of life. The paradigms that are created in childhood will powerfully influence our decisions, values, and lifestyles for as long as we live. Freudian analysis dominated the field of psychotherapy until relatively recently.

Carl Jung operated with a different understanding of the process of human development. While denying none of the importance of childhood issues, Jung believed that, at different stages of life, different issues arise. Life is not a matter of just running downhill from childhood; it is a matter of dealing with the different issues that present themselves at the various stages of our lives.

Among other things, Jung believed that midlife was the "noontime" of life, not the beginning of the "over-the-hill" time of life suggested by the black-draped birthday cards you purchase for your friend who is turning forty. Jung's view of midlife would be closer to the "life begins at forty" slogan. At midlife, one is not just dealing with the issues of childhood, but with a whole new dimension of life, with a new set of priorities and issues.

Jungian psychologists believe that in every stage of our lives we *express* parts of ourselves and we *suppress* other parts. As I understand them, they believe that in the second half of life we *express* what we have *suppressed* in the first half of life, and we *suppress* what we have *expressed*. This is undoubtedly why people often claim that they suddenly do not understand a midlife person. Parents tell me they do not understand their forty-two-year-old daughter. "She was always so neat and organized. She was a stay-at-home mother.

And she was such a genteel lady. And now she's dating a man with no manners, her house is not picked up, and she is going to bars, which she never did before."

Likewise, I often hear the spouse or family of a man wonder if he is mentally ill because he is engaging in behavior that is absolutely the opposite of what it has been since they have known him. An obsessed workaholic, he has suddenly begun to smell the flowers. He is talking about leaving his position at the top of his career and opening a small business of his own. An almost neurotic saver of money, he has begun spending it wildly, or so it seems.

Author Mark Gerzon puts it this way: "As we age we human beings yearn for wholeness ... we yearn to live our unlived lives."[1] That is, that part of us that has been hidden deep within us strives for expression. That part may have been hidden from our conscious mind or it may have been there all along as a dream or phantasy we were afraid to express. Or we may have been allowing the expectations of others to become demands to which we acquiesced. And now we want to live that which we have been afraid to live, to express that which we were afraid to express before because of the disapproval of family, friends, or business associates.

"All my life", Mona says, "I have been the person my mother wanted me to be. I kept house the way she kept house. I cooked what she cooked. I joined the clubs that she picked out. I even dressed the way she thought I should. I can't do that any more. I have to be me. And mother will just have to get used to it. I want to start living my life before I get any older."

Mona's theme is one that I hear quite often. In midlife there is a sense that we are indeed getting older. I do not so much hear a fear of dying, but rather a fear of not living one's life before one dies. That's the issue. There is a very real, but new sense of self that asserts itself at midlife. Or as Gerzon says,

---

[1] Mark Gerzon, *Listening to Midlife: Turning Your Crisis into a Quest* (Boston: Shambala, 1996), 5.

"Now we yearn for wholeness."[1] And we cannot be "whole" unless and until the unlived, unexpressed parts of the self find expression.

I must confess that sometimes midlife behavior looks a lot like adolescent rebellion. Mona's parents certainly think of it in that way. And they blame it on the man she is dating, just as the parents of adolescents blame that rebellion on their adolescent son's or daughter's girlfriend/boyfriend. I believe that there *are* similarities between adolescence and midlife. Both are times when persons are concerned with identity issues. "Just who am I, anyway?" Or as I sometimes rephrase the question for them, "Who would you *like* to be at this point in your life?" I can even say that, as a result of working more and more with people in midlife, I have come to the conclusion that midlife changes seem to be more dramatic in the lives of persons who were not at all rebellious as teenagers. This is not based on any research I have done, nor am I aware of any research that may prove or disprove my limited, but I think legitimate, observation.

I agree with Murray Stein, author of *In Midlife, A Jungian Perspective*, who says, "Adulthood is [just] as developmental as childhood or adolescence . . . in all of life we are in psychological process and therefore subject to internal flux and change."[2] Just think once more about the turbulence of your own adolescence or that of your children. It is a little bit shocking to think that midlife is anything like going through adolescence again. My experience says it is, though I admit that, at least for most persons, it may be a lot quieter. But while it is quieter, it is also much deeper. By midlife we are a lot more mature. We have a lot more experiences that we have lived through. We are wiser. And we are a lot more in control of our lives than when we were teenagers. Murray Stein calls midlife "a crisis of the spirit" in which "old selves are lost and new ones come into being."[3]

---

[1] Ibid.
[2] Murray Stein, *In Midlife: A Jungian Perspective* (Dallas: Spring Publications, 1983), 2.
[3] Ibid., 3.

So when is midlife? Most authorities I read say it begins somewhere between forty and forty-five. I have no argument with locating the beginning of midlife in the late forties, but some of the emotional and psychological phenomena associated with midlife may not become conscious issues until the mid-to late fifties. Most people seem to be past their midlife issues by the time they reach the age of sixty. It may not be helpful, however, to associate midlife with a particular age; perhaps it is more revealing to consider some of the moods, attitudes, feelings, and expressions that are actually a part of the phenomenon called *midlife*. Here are some typical examples.

- *"I feel like I am running out of gas."* This is from a forty-six year-old woman, married with three children. She was married at age twenty to her high school boyfriend. Her youngest child, a daughter, is sixteen. She has worked part-time for most of her married life. Between homemaking, child-rearing and part-time employment, she has had little time for herself; she has not been seriously unhappy. She considers herself a good mother and a good wife, but all of her life has been devoted to seeing to it that others "got what they needed." She says, "it feels like I have been running on empty for the last year," and now that the youngest is about to leave home she wants to know how she can be energized once again.

- *"Is this all there is?"* This came from a man who has gradually climbed the corporate ladder over the years. He has gotten at least one step farther than he thought he would, and he is puzzled because he thought he should be experiencing a tremendous sense of accomplishment. "I don't know what exactly I expected, but I expected something more satisfying that what I am experiencing. Was I fooling myself all this time? I have sacrificed a lot to get where I am. I have not been the greatest of fathers, but I believed sincerely the best thing I could do for my kids was to get to the top so that I could give them what they needed. I feel emotionally disconnected to them instead. I'm not even very close to my wife. So here I am, at the place I thought would give me so much happiness. But I'm not happy, and worse, I feel lonely as hell."

• *"I don't know who I am anymore."* I heard this expression separately from a woman and from a man on the same day. I'll take the woman first. She was a fifty-year-old woman whose husband had just informed her that he wanted a divorce. She knew that the marriage had not been that close for some time, but she figured her marriage was just going through a phase, like that of some of her close friends, a group of women who enjoyed a number of different activities together. She admitted that over the years his activities and her activities never seemed to come together. In recent years he had gotten into jogging and occasionally nagged her about the lack of demanding exercise in her life, but he didn't seem to make a big issue about it. She had adjusted to his workaholic tendencies. He left for the office at 6:00 A.M. and did not get home until after 7:00 in the evening. She is concerned that there may be another woman. (There was, a woman who was into jogging.) Facing life,and facing the future outside the marriage are scary realities. It is even scarier to her to discover that she really doesn't know who she is outside her marriage.

The man who spoke the same sentence has lost his position as the result of restructuring at his company. He has just celebrated his fiftieth birthday. He has been at the same company for twenty years and in the same career since graduating from college. He has been given a very generous settlement from the company, but he is almost paralyzed about the future. He has defined himself by his work all these years, and he is a typical American male in that respect. He has said (and note where the emphasis is), "I *am* an engineer." His identity has been defined by his career, which is why, without the career, he doesn't know who he is anymore.

What is important about the man and woman above is that they illustrate something I believe is important about midlife and the impact it has on marriage. I believe that men and women are socialized differently in America, and this in spite of the considerable strength of the women's movement and the growing men's movement. Men are socialized to find their chief identity and satisfaction in life from their work and achievements; women are socialized to find their chief identity and satisfaction from their intimate connections.

But at midlife everything changes. At midlife a man begins to have more and more difficulty finding his identity and meaning in life from his work. And at midlife , a woman begins to have more and more difficulty finding her identity and meaning in life from her intimate connections. A man slowly begins to become conscious of his need for more intimate connections; a woman likewise begins to become conscious of a need to achieve something in the career arena. So men and women in midlife are in the process of exchanging the primary arenas in which each will seek meaning and significance. He moves from the achievement arena to the intimacy arena as she moves from intimacy to achievement.

Sally was a middle aged woman. She had raised three children and nursed a mother-in-law until death. Her marriage has not been a happy one for many years. Then, at age fifty-one she decided to go to college. Her husband was irate. He refused to approve of her doing what to him was clearly a "damn fool thing to do." I asked her how important it was to her to go to college. She wondered why I would ask such a question, and I replied that I was sure that if it was important enough to her, her husband would go along. She indicated that it was very important to her. Sally had never worked outside the home and wanted to go to college to pick up some office skills, thinking that she might like to do office work. I worked with Sally on raising her level of self-differentiation from her husband, something she had never done. This is accomplished by becoming very clear about what you think, what you want to do, and what you do not want to do; you then follow through regardless of the emotional anxiety it raises in your family. All this is done while staying connected to your family, however; in this case, to her husband. In the past, Sally would back off as soon as her husband got irritated or mad, wanting to keep peace with him at all costs. This time she did not back down. Sally went to college, and the couple is still together. Sally has enjoyed the experience of achieving the mastery of college courses in keyboarding and office management. She does not believe her marriage will ever be happier than it has been, but she has decided she will stay in the marriage; she thinks divorce and living alone would be the worse of two evils.

When she came to see me, Sally was a typical midlife woman who had gotten as far as she believed she could go in the intimacy arena and wanted to achieve something in the other arena. Indeed she felt that something important deep within her would die if she did not follow through. I suggested she read the book *The Hero Within: Six Archetypes We Live By*, by Carol Pearson; she read it in a couple of days. Pearson describes and explains six of the Jungian "archetypes" in her book—Innocent, Orphan, Martyr, Wanderer, Warrior, and Magician. Sally came to see me as soon as she finished the book, and her first words were, "Why did you want me to read that book?" I told her I would answer her question, but I would like her to answer one of my questions first: "What did you learn from reading the book?" She said, "That I have lived most of my life in the Martyr role and that I am wanting to be The Wanderer. My reply was, "That's why I wanted you to read the book; I was concerned that you might stay in that Martyr mode for the rest of your life." I am convinced that something deep inside this woman *would* have died. That something is what gives us our vitality and zest for life. Some would call it the soul.

In this book then, I agree with the notion that, at midlife, there is a powerful internal force that seeks correction and balance. That correction may involve a profound change in both values and lifestyle. What we have neglected demands attention. What we have suppressed demands expression. What we have forgotten demands to be remembered. I am also presupposing the validity of Jungian archetypes while admitting that I am no expert in explaining them; but there clearly are roles, paradigms, or patterns by which we live, and these paradigms and patterns clearly seem to shift in midlife.

Whether we shift our paradigms or our spouses do, however, the point is that this will have a profound effect upon our relationship. If we begin to *express* what we previously have *suppressed*, it will clearly have an affect upon our relationships. In all relationships, but especially in the marriage relationship we develop and grow in tandem, in a kind of mutuality. The "me" that I develop is a "me" that must get along with "you." So if I change, you will have to make some kind of adaptation; and if you change, I will have to adapt. Over the years, these mutual adaptations take on clear patterns. The patterns become grooves, paths that we walk together in mutual adaptation. And then comes midlife. People jump out of the grooves; they throw away the patterns and begin to develop new ones. Suddenly, even though there may be a twenty- or thirty-year history, it seems that we are in unfamiliar territory. The maps we have been using for each other no longer work. New maps must be drawn. New patterns must be followed. New ways of relating must be worked out. The self that I became adjusted to is changing, and therefore my adjustment has to keep changing, too. We have to hit a moving target.

Chapter Two
Marriage and Relationships
at Midlife

If we accept my belief that a powerful internal force appears at midlife which seeks correction and balance is true, the obvious next question is: How does the shifting associated with midlife affect marriages at and beyond midlife? The answer is that in our culture, there is an apparent increase in both the incidence of marital problems and the incidence of divorce later in marriage. There was a time when couples who had celebrated their twenty-fifth wedding anniversary seldom if ever got a divorce, but that is not the case today. We are witnessing a disturbing increase in the incidence of divorce after twenty and twenty-five years of marriage.

FACTORS THAT CONTRIBUTE TO DIVORCE AT MIDLIFE

Currently about eleven percent of all divorces take place after twenty years of marriage. I believe that percentage will rise in the next several decades; but even if the percentage does not go up, the sheer number of divorces will increase since, beginning in the year 2010, the number of people in the midlife category (forty to sixty) will almost double.

Most all of the research continues to show that there is an inverse relationship between the duration of a marriage and the probability of divorce, which means that the longer a marriage lasts the less likely it is that divorce will occur. That inverse relationship is not as strong as it once was, however, and I predict that unless we do something different, it will become weaker yet. Why is this? I believe the answer to that question is complicated, which is to suggest that a number of factors are contributing to this higher incidence of divorce for people later in life.

People Live Longer

Certainly one would have to cite the fact that many people are living longer, which gives more time for problems to come to the surface or to become more aggravating. Because people are living longer, they are more inclined to take steps to eliminate causes of unhappiness.

Children Leave Home

One of the chief reasons couples stay together earlier in life disappears with the aging of the marriage, namely the children. By the twenty-fifth year of marriage, most of the children have either left home or are nearly ready to do so. People who may have been reluctant to divorce because of the harm done to the children are no longer as reluctant. In my practice I continue to see an impressive number of couples who are divorcing when the last child is in the last year of high school or already in college.

Women's Education and Independence

Compared to a century ago, many women today are *relatively* more educated and more independent, and therefore less inclined to stay in a marriage that is not fulfilling. I am well aware that divorce results in a definite financial hardship for women of any age and education, but it is still quite different from my maternal grandmothers' day. My mother's mother had a high school education, and if she had been divorced, she would have had to work at something related to her homemaking skills. When she was left a widow at a young age, she found employment as a maid in a large hotel. Today, although it is still a definite hardship, many women are already working full time or can, with some remedial education, either return to a career they had earlier or train for a new career altogether. Age, however, can play a crucial role in how practical that may be.

Factors such as the wife's education, which act as a deterrent to divorce earlier in the marriage, are more positively related to a higher incidence of divorce in later life. Early in the marriage, the college education of a wife seems to prevent divorce, but this is not so in later life. This suggests that the more educated a woman is, the less likely she is to stay in an unhappy marriage.

Influence of Popular Culture

There has been a tremendous increase in the number of divorced men and women portrayed positively on television and in the movies. These people are seen as happy and successful; they have recovered from a previously unhappy relationship and are living fuller lives than ever before.

Better Health

I would like to suggest that the improving health status of Americans is an additional factor. In past generations, significant health problems present by the time a marriage got to twenty-five years may have had the effect of increasing dependency on the other spouse. Changes in lifestyle, as well as improvements in health care, have made it possible for people in their fifties and sixties to be much less troubled with debilitating conditions than they were several decades ago.

The Cumulative Effect

A final factor, I strongly insist, is the cumulative effect of negative indicators that have been present from the beginning. Let me give you some examples of what I mean. Marriage during the teen years is a clear predictor of divorce. Many of these marriages dissolve within the first five years of the marriage, but many survive to twenty or twenty-five years. The risks for divorce

associated with teenage marriage do not simply disappear, however; the negative consequences are still there, but may not lead to the actual divorce until
later. The problems that have always been there have been endured, but for
many the willingness to endure seems to disappear at midlife. I have observed
women who have lived with a husband who has been a workaholic since the
first year of marriage, but at midlife she is less inclined to endure it and she
leaves the marriage. Or a man who has always resented his wife's spending
habits, often in silence, will no longer tolerate them at midlife. There is thus a
cumulative effect of marital problems, particularly when they are not discussed or dealt with. They seem to reach a critical mass at midlife and will no
longer be tolerated. All of this seems to fit with what the Jungians tell us about
midlife—what is suppressed in the first half of life is expressed in the second
half. For marriage, that seems to mean that what is tolerated and/or accepted
in the early years may not be tolerated later. What a spouse may have been
silent about comes up and is expressed, sometimes loudly.

My conclusion, then, is that since people are living longer, and since the
lives they are living are healthier, they are determined to have some quality
both in their lives and in their relationships.

The evidence for the truth of what I have described above comes from the
stories I hear from people in my counseling office. By *story*, I mean the answer
I get when I ask the question, "Tell me what the problem is with your marriage from your perspective. What went wrong?" In the following chapter we
will listen to some of those stories.

Chapter Three

Perspectives on Marriage and Relationships at Midlife

MIDLIFE STORIES

In the stories that follow there is always a core rationale. While more than one issue is involved, after thinking and fretting about their marriage many of my clients feel they have a core perspective that seems to be both the key to their unhappiness and the reason they have chosen to dissolve their marriage. Here are the ones that I hear the most frequently.

"This marriage was flawed from the beginning."

I have been surprised by the number of people who have told me that they knew on the day of their wedding that the marriage was not going to work. Gloria even told me that she put a note on the front door of the church saying that the rehearsal and wedding were canceled due to "unforseen circumstances," but that her mother tore the note down and told her she was going to go through with the wedding because too much money had already been spent. Another woman, Judy, told me that while she was walking down the aisle with her father, she was aware that Forrest, the man she was marrying, pleased her father very much but was not her first choice at all. She felt that because her father was older and perhaps wiser, she should go ahead. This man might be right after all, and somewhere down the line she would appreciate him a lot more; he had some very good qualities, all of which had been pointed out to her by her father. But she was marrying him because he was Dad's choice, not hers.

Other flawed marriages start out as forced. A bride is pregnant, and the groom is the father; and someone has told them that "this is the right thing to do so that the baby will have both a father and a mother." My frank assessment of an unwanted and premarital pregnancy is that it constitutes a problem for which all of the answers are bad. The divorce rate for such forced marriages is very high; and when the wedding occurs in the teen years, half of the couples do not make it to their first anniversary. This is another case of what I described earlier as a cumulative problem, namely that the couple does the "right thing" by getting married, but once the child is ready to leave home the reality that brought them together has run its course. Many of these marriages that somehow manage to hold together until midlife come apart then. A marriage that is flawed from the start will just not get better on its own.

For some people, the consciousness that a marriage is not a good match may come later, but still quite early on, within the first five years. "He promised he would cut down on his drinking after the wedding, but by the end of the first year, it was obvious that that was not the case. It got even worse." "She promised that she would not be such a clothes horse after the wedding, but nothing changed." I am always amazed that ninety-percent of the problems that become serious issues later in a marriage are clearly visible in the courtship, but apparently not taken seriously. They are still problems, however, and they come up twenty and even thirty years later. Some people stay in these flawed-from-the-beginning marriages because of parental and family pressure, some because of their religious commitments; still others because they believe it may get better down the line. By midlife they are ready to give up. They know it will not get any better, and hope for any change has died.

"We have just grown farther and farther apart over the years."
Or as some midlife people phrase it, we are growing in different directions. Certainly it must be recognized that all of life involves growth, and that the nature and direction of this growth depends on a number of factors. Our life-experiences influence the direction of our growth and it would be helpful if we could clearly and accurately predict which of these experiences will be growth producing and which will not. Twenty years ago I found myself telling couples that while relationship partners do not have to share every life experience—that would be impossible—it is important that they share those experiences that are "growth producing." I soon realized, however, that one could not always predict which experiences these would be.

How could John have known that the three-day conference he attended would result in a passionate new interest in a newly developing field of law, and that within six months he would be involved in a new career that would consume his attention and energy for the next ten years. The experience literally made John a new man; as he puts it, "it gave me a whole new purpose for my existence." That's growth producing. Over the next few years, John would become a much more people-oriented person than the man that Andrea married. Ten years down the line from that fateful conference it seemed to Andrea that so much about John had developed in a different direction that he was not the same man she expected him to be. John's politics, his values, and even his religious affiliation *had* changed; he was now interested in a lifestyle that Andrea was not.

I do not mean to suggest that all growth "in different directions" is as dramatic as it was for John and Andrea. Most of the time, what created distance between two spouses occurs in such tiny increments that it cannot be detected on a week-to-week or month-to-month basis, but ten years down the line it can be seen quite clearly.

There is, however, a typical pattern in America. During courtship, most American lovers seem to really work at their relationship, investing significant amounts of time and energy in it. They both experience that each is a priority to the other. Especially in the beginning of the courtship, they spend a lot of time in conversation. They talk for hours and do a lot of things together. Most couples do not continue the patterns they established in courtship, however. Indeed, it is not even possible. What we see in the typical pattern is that men shift their primary investment of time and energy to work and career. Women also shift to their careers and to the home, at least until the first child is born. Then when many women go back to work, they shift the primary investment to children and the home, and sandwich their career in as best they can. In fact, most working women in America are tremendously overburdened just because they have to juggle so many demands at the same time. My point is simply that, for a variety of reasons, a primary focus on the couple's relationship is not a high priority since they focus somewhere else. While I know that focusing on children and home upkeep are necessary, I do not believe that it is necessary that the focus on the marriage relationship should be placed at the bottom of the list.

I am also not suggesting that women should give up careers when children are born. A woman's career is just as important to her own overall satisfaction in life as a man's career is to his. What I want to suggest is that both need to make adjustments in their careers, both need to share the burdens of parenthood and home care so that both can still keep some of the focus on their relationship. I have pointedly said to couples with whom I work in premarital education that the birth of the first child is a major event in the history of their marriage. There are many marriages that jump the tracks in the period between the onset of pregnancy and a time up to eighteen months after delivery, and never get back on track. I am even so bold to suggest that, with the exception of the first three or four months after a child's birth, a couple should not allow children to "come first" in their family. I believe that the children should come second, careers should come third, and the relationship should come first.

My reason for this almost anti-American point of view is that parenthood does not hold families together, the parents' relationship does. If that relationship goes down the tubes, the family is coming apart. The overall health and functioning of a family is only as good or functional as the overall functioning of the relationship. I will even argue that neglected and dysfunctional relationships have enormous negative effects upon careers. I once proposed to a medium-sized corporation that it would be in their best interests to provide marital education to their employees. I was told that they were already devoting all the time and financial resources to alcohol and drug rehabilitation and could not allow more time off or pay for such education. I wondered that no one had apparently asked whether or not marital or family dysfunction might be playing a significant role in the development of alcohol and drug problems. Treating only the alcohol and drug behavior is, in my mind, treating the symptom, and not the cause. Many corporations have discovered the cost-effectiveness of providing fitness facilities and coaches for their employees. I'm all for it. But I am also convinced that "fit relationships" would also be found to be cost-effective.

I am proposing that it is crucial to keep the focus on every phase of the relationship. Anything that threatens or disrupts that focus is a threat to the health and integrity of the family. One of the places where this can be seen is in families that are struck by tragedy or by some phenomenon that powerfully changes the focus. Families that experience the death of a child are put into such a situation, when one or both parents are in such deep grief that the focus on their relationship is lost. The divorce rate for these families is very high. Another example is when a child with a disability is born into a family. My wife, Jo, has worked with families with exceptional children for over twenty years, and about ten years ago she suggested that I ought to adapt some of my notions about love and marriage and address the special marital stresses of families with exceptional children. I was amazed to discover that the divorce rate for these marriages was six times as high as the national average, but now

I understand why. An exceptional child demands exceptional care, care that is often demanding and energy-depleting. The more profound the handicap, the more focus on the child is required, and the less focus, energy, and time there is for the couple's relationship. Mothers of these children typically get focused on the child. Fathers get focused on their jobs because paying the extra bills now requires attention to increasing the family income. The relationship begins to suffer.

I can often see clearly, by hindsight, other crucial turning points in a relationship. What made those turning points crucial was that they had a profound effect upon the focus of one or both of the spouses. From that point on, the growth of each person began moving in different directions, or a distance began developing which, by midlife, would be threatening to the marriage.

"I/he/she changed."

The emphasis of this perspective is not so much on a growth process developing slowly over a period of years. Instead, the emphasis here is on the end result of a process in which one person sees the other as a very different person, or experiences the other person as quite different, from the person who got married many years before.

"I realize that I am the one who has changed," confesses Haylie. "He is the same person that he was when we got married, but I am a different person. My values are not the same. What I want out of life is completely different. I don't see life or myself the same way as I did when I met Tom and we got married." Tom is a special sales representative for a large corporation. He is very successful, and the lifestyle he can provide for Haylie and the children is definitely upscale. They have recently added an in-ground swimming pool, and the children are looking forward to swimming parties with their friends in the summer. Tom and Haylie had talked about their life goals and plans when they were courting and during the first couple of years of marriage.

They were on the same track, but they are not any more. The upscale lifestyle is not only not a goal for Haylie, she really sees that lifestyle as contrary to the kind of happiness she wants. Tom does not understand what has happened, but agrees that Haylie is a different person. The woman who enjoyed country-club life and a glamorous lifestyle is no longer interested. She is into new-age spirituality, recycling is an obsession, and she sends letters all over the country to warn about global warming. What is worse, Tom realizes that Haylie doesn't really even like him anymore, and he is tired of defending a way of life that he believes he and the children are entitled to because he has worked so hard and so long to achieve it. He has been hoping that this is just a phase that she is going through and that one of these days she will get off "this crazy kick."

This change started with a workshop Haylie attended. Then she read a book. Then another workshop. More importantly, I think, Haylie is a midlife woman. She admits to a vague feeling of being "unfulfilled" with her life. No big trauma; no dramatic experiences. As she works through her own life, she sees her "earlier self" as kind of self-centered and naïve about life. She calls herself an "unconscious sponge," just absorbing whatever she can about life. She sees herself as never having been very serious about life. She is afraid her children are developing the same way that she did, shallow and self-centered. And that is how she has come to see Tom. "I realize that I am the one who has changed. It's kind of unfair to Tom, I suppose. He is succeeding just the way he planned, and the "old me" enjoyed that at one time. I can't any more, and I don't think Tom can change. In fact he has made it clear that he doesn't even want to. He just wants me to come to my senses. I have a hard time explaining to him that this is exactly what's happened. I have come to my senses."

Haylie is a midlife woman, and she has changed. It is more than intellectual, more than emotional. It is a deep spiritual change. She does not call it a religious change, but she has become more serious about religion and the church even though for years she gave little attention to that aspect of her life.

Now the spiritual part of who she is demands attention, satisfaction, and a chance to develop. But she realizes that the future involves a "journey that Tom cannot make with me." In fact, Tom could make that journey with her, but he does not want to. Haylie has changed into a person whom Tom frankly does not like, a "new-age person with her head in the clouds." He too is concerned about the children and does not want them to turn into "the flower children of the nineties."

Am I saying that the growth of one person will doom a marriage or a long-term relationship? Absolutely not. Not necessarily. There are many factors that determine whether growth will have a strengthening or weakening affect upon the relationship. These include the direction of the growth, the depth of the growth, and how effectively two people communicate on an ongoing basis in their relationship. But growth is necessary. We grow or we die; it's that simple. In all growth there is risk, but in all growth there is also adventure, and challenge.

Let me add quickly that not all change is due to the growth that is a part of what we call human development through the life cycle. There is also change that is due to trauma or disease. Consider the story of Clark and Brenda, a couple in their early forties with three children. When they first came to see me, Brenda complained that Clark was increasingly obsessive about sex and seemed to not hear her when she would say no. She experienced that as a lack of respect, and felt that he was another man who just would not listen. In the course of doing their marital history, I also heard that Clark had changed jobs recently and noted that Brenda was more than a little upset about how much she could depend on him as a coprovider for the family.

Since Clark had a history of working since he was in high school, I wondered why she should doubt his ability to continue his share of the providing. That's when I heard that he had lost several jobs in the last five years and that he sometimes found a new job quickly enough, but took one with less salary. What was the problem? Clark indicated that, to him, the reason for his being let go always seemed to be personal. What exactly had he heard on his last evaluation? He said he was falsely accused of talking too much. Other employees complained that he was a "motor mouth." Since that sounded a little bit like something Brenda had been talking about with his obsessive petitions for sex and his apparently not hearing, or respecting, her "no" I asked a simple question. "Clark have you ever had a head injury?" The answer was "yes." My next question was "when?" It had occurred when he was in his last year of college, but he insisted it was no big deal; he had recovered completely. I am not a doctor, and don't even want to play doctor, but I did ask if he was unconscious for any length of time as a result of that accident. He was indeed, for almost a week!

I asked about follow-up after he was released from the hospital. Clark became a little frustrated with my suggesting that something as old as that accident could have any significance in his life at the present time, but I was deeply concerned that there were no follow-up appointments with a neurologist after he was released from the hospital. He told me that there could not have been any significant consequences because he had gone on to finish college and get his degree. He had a teaching certificate and had taught in high school. Brenda chimed in at this point that he did finish college, but that his mother and sister had done his term papers after the accident. I referred Clark to a neurologist for a work-up, which showed a that a spot as big as a dime in his frontal lobe was dead tissue. Clark was a changed man; he had a permanent brain injury. Now suddenly both the problems he was having with job evaluations and the problem with his apparent inability to hear Brenda' pleas made made sense. This and other problems related to that brain injury had brought Brenda to the point that she was ready to leave the marriage, but after discovering the real cause of Clark's behavior, she changed her mind. They are now dealing with the situation from a completely different perspective. So there are changes resulting from injury or disease than can also result in someone discovering that his or her spouse is a different person.

"The only thing holding me in this marriage was the children. "
This particular story is told by both men and women, but more often by
women. The belief left unexpressed in this story is that it is best for children
to grow up in a home where their biological parents are present. You would
have a hard time finding anyone who would argue against that idea, but I
would add two caveats. First, I do not think it is good for children to grow up
in a home where there is physical violence and abuse, even if that home has
both biological parents present. There will be negative consequences from
divorce, I know, but staying in a marriage where there is violence may have a
terminal consequence. In addition, there is a comprehensive consensus that
children who grow up with domestic violence as a part of their daily routine
are violent themselves as adults. Violence should never be tolerated for any
reason, not even "for the sake of the kids."

My other caveat is that I think some families are so severely dysfunctional
that children are damaged every bit as much as in physically abusive situations. Wallerstein and Kelly, in their book *Surviving The Breakup*, impressed
me with their conclusion that we have underestimated the damage done to
both children and adults as a result of divorce. But I also believe that if they
had been studying children from severely dysfunctional families, they would
have concluded that we have also underestimated the damage done within
these families.

I deliberately use the term *severely dysfunctional* because I do not think
that a *moderate* unhappiness is dysfunctional. By severely disfunctional I am
thinking of the family in which there is chronic conflict and loud and verbally
abusive language that goes on all the time. I am thinking of the family invaded by major depressive disorder, or in which adults have chronic addiction to alcohol or other substances and refuse to get help. I believe we need to
be aware that when we ask children, as children, whether they will give their
approval to the parents getting a divorce, they will decline their approval.
When we ask those same people, years later, as adults, they express the clear

conviction that they wish their parents had gotten a divorce. Frankly, I believe that growing up in a severely dysfunctional family does just as much long-term damage to children as growing up in a family affected by divorce.

Thus, while I have a certain amount of admiration for people who do tough it out until the children are grown, I believe that it is difficult to prove that this is always better for children. It is better for a spouse to demand that his or her partner either get some counseling or the relationship will be terminated. I should add, that parents are mistaken if they believe that their children will have no emotional problems if they wait to divorce until the children are grown. I have seen plenty of adult children in their twenties and thirties have a very difficult time with their parents' divorce, especially if there is a subsequent re-marriage. In some cases, the emotional reactivity of adult children is quite severe.

"I have come to the realization that I have not been living my own life. I've been living my (fill in the blank)'s life."

Many different persons may be found in the blank. Certainly parents, mother, or father are the ones inserted most often, but it might be an older sibling, a deceased sibling, or a life prescribed by a grandparent, teacher, minister, or coach. It can be any person who is in a position to be so powerful that a child gives up his or her individuality because he or she either is afraid to oppose the controller or has not developed enough ego strength to do it.

I don't know who coined the term *self-differentiation*, but I first read it in the writings of Murry Bowen. Bowen, a medical doctor, was a pioneer in systems theory applied to the functioning of family systems. A highly self-differentiated person can do several things:

- Distinguish between thinking and feeling.
- Remain relatively nonreactive in an anxious environment.
- Be able to assert an "I" when the group demands "we."
- Articulate clearly what he or she thinks, believes, will do, and follow through in the face of pressure to believe, do, or think what the group wants.

- Stay connected to everyone in the group even while disagreeing.
- Accept total responsibility for his or her own emotional well-being.

There are three times (at least) in every person's life, I think, when the pressure to self-differentiate asserts itself. The first is at the age of about eighteen months, by which time we have learned two of the most powerful words in human vocabulary. The first is "I," and the second is "no."

The second time nature presents this pressure is during adolescence. This is what is behind the opposition and rebellion so characteristic of that age group, but I do not want readers to think that self-differentiation is rebellion. What most adolescents are doing is experimenting with some of their own feelings and thoughts, and they are testing these out in relation to the values and lifestyles of their parents. When children's experimentation with new ways of thinking and alternative values raises the anxiousness of their parents, and the parents react, that reaction may result in rebellion.

The third time in life when the urge to self-differentiate comes into play is, of course, at midlife. As a result, when I hear someone tell me that they believe that they have not been living their life but someone else's, I take it seriously. In fact, in the counseling sessions with that person I want to help him or her find out who in the system needs to be dealt with in order to accomplish a higher level of self-differentiation. And I emphasize "a higher level." I do not give people the impression that we can all be perfectly self-differentiated. According to Dr. Bowen, each family system probably imposes some limits on how self-differentiated any one person within that system may be, and no one in the family is likely to go beyond that limit. But I believe it is possible for people to raise their self-differentiation level. I also believe that the level of self-differentiation one can achieve in, say, the work environment, may be higher than in another environment, such as the family.

All of us know very well individuals who have been so dominated by a strong father or mother that they behave as though every major decision they make must have mother's or father's approval. I knew a highly educated and successful (in his career, anyway) man in his mid-forties whose mother still picked out all his clothes. And I can remember going home with a friend from school for a weekend—we were probably eighteen at the time—and he insisted that his mother come with him to buy his shoes. He was afraid to make the choice on his own.

More often, though, we see the phenomenon of low self-differentiation in the person who is never responsible for his or her own choices, problems, and fate. Somebody else is always to blame; they are merely the victims of someone else's bad advice, or victims of fate.

Whenever I talk about self-differentiation, I believe it is also important to make clear what is not self-differentiation. Opposition is not self-differentiation. Adolescents who loudly and angrily oppose their parents' rules, and values often do not, or cannot, oppose the values and "rules" of their peer group. Peer pressure is as dominant as any parent, and children who allow themselves to be swayed by it are very poorly self-differentiated. Pay attention sometime to the pressure that peers can bring on someone who will not conform to the peer group. They can make a teenager's life a lot more difficult than can most parents. The pressure to conform, by the way, is an indicator of the anxiety level of the peer group. Anxious systems do not like self-differentiated members.

Cutting yourself off from your family is also not self-differentiation; distance and silence do not change the emotional connections. Darrel was a young man in his early twenties. He came for counseling because of the dominance of his father, a very controlling man. His mother and father were divorced and, according to Darrel, it was because his mother could no longer tolerate her controlling husband. Darrel believed that since the divorce his father's efforts to control his life had gotten worse. His solution was to go to a college as far away as he could so that his father could not "get to me." He had been thinking about Alaska. I challenged Darrel to work on his relationship with his father no matter where he decided to go to college, and that working on the relationship with his controlling father would not only benefit that relationship but all the other relationships in his life. "You don't know my father," he said; and, as far as I know, he moved to Alaska.

Angela had a different story. Although Angela is not a midlife woman, her story provides a good illustration of an important aspect of personal growth in self-differentiation. Angela's mother had died when she was a little girl. Her father had remarried about five years later. Angela's stepmother was very supportive of Angela in her attempts to keep a controlling father at bay. When she came to see me, she was terrified that her father would find out that she had dropped all her classes except one, and that what she really wanted to do was drop out of school and work in retail clothing for a while before she went back to school. Her stepmother knew about this, and the two were keeping it a secret from her father. Secrets in family systems are not healthy.

It was clear that Angela missed her mother. She had seen enough of her parents' marriage that she knew her mother had to deal with Dad's controlling dominance too. If only Mother were still around so she could talk about this problem with her. I gave Angela the assignment of writing a letter to her mother, and telling her about how she was feeling, about her fear of her father's anger, and about her frustration of not being able to take control of her own life. She wrote a beautiful letter. It was obvious that she was very clear about what she was thinking, what she believed, and what she wanted to do. I then asked her to write the letter she wished she could receive from her mother in response to her letter. With her permission, I saved that letter, with all the names blacked out. It is one of the most touching letters I have ever read.

"Now you are ready to face your father," I told her. I showed her how in the letter it was clear that she had internalized her mother. The advice from her mother was mature and responsible. She told me that it was with great fear and trembling that she went to speak with her father. She asked him not to stop her until she was finished, and he agreed. Much to her surprise, she did not get the blast of anger she expected. (I think that is because she was so clear about what she thought, felt, believed, and wanted to do.) She didn't get an unqualified blessing either. He had many questions and doubts about the direction she wanted to go, but she experienced the session as one in which she got permission to live her own life. In her last session with me, as she left my office, she turned to me and said, "I feel like a book that's just been opened." I took that as one of the best compliments a counselor can get from a client.

If you decide at some point in your life that someone else has been running it (which really means that you have been allowing someone else to run it) and you now want to take over, it does not necessarily mean the end of your marriage or relationship. Even though some people have been poorly self-differentiated for many years, it does not mean that they chose a spouse with whom they cannot be quite compatible. The problem is that many people replace a dominating parent with a dominating spouse. Once a person has lived with a dominating spouse for many years, becoming more self-differentiated will indeed change the dynamics of a marriage; but I would still argue that it does not necessarily mean that one will have to leave the marriage. Remember that being more self-differentiated does not mean disconnecting from others in your system. You do not accomplish personal growth just by divorcing a dominant spouse; you can grow by staying with a dominant spouse and refusing to be dominated. I am assuming of course, that this dominance does not involve any physical threat or violence. There is no doubt the marriage will be a lot more uncomfortable during the time it takes for a dominant spouse to adapt to the new reality; but if that spouse wants to continue the relationship he or she will have to adapt.

~

All the information I have presented to this point leads me to conclude that what has kept a marriage together in the first half of life will probably not be effective for the second half. New strategies must be developed to meet the new demands that each partner brings to the midlife relationship.

It is also clear that if new strategies must be developed, these strategies must be negotiated by both partners. Betty Carter and Monica McGoldrick, in their comprehensive book, *The Changing Family Life Cycle: A Framework for Family Therapy*, identify the child-launching stage, when children leave home and move toward greater independence, as the critical time for relationship renewal to begin. They suggest that between the launching of the first and the last child, the couple needs to complete the development of new strategies that will carry their relationship through the second half of life.

The obvious next question is, "How do I go about this?" And just as importantly, "What exactly does a quality relationship look like?" Is there some kind of template or model that can be used as a reference point in the task of renewal? I turn to that subject in the next two chapters.

Part Two

Love at Midlife

Chapter Four
What a Loving Relationship Looks Like

The American Model of Love

What does a loving relationship look like? This is the fundamental question that must be answered whether you are a midlife person, an eighteen-year-old high school senior, or a thirty-year-old woman or man. The universal demand is to be loved. But how will I know if I am being loved well? And what do I do to love another person well? I believe people want to love and want to be loved, but most people do not have a clear and understandable picture of what a loving relationship looks like. What is needed is some kind of a model, paradigm, or norm that we can use, a template we can hold up against our experience to tell us the quality of loving we are getting or giving.

I won't suggest for a minute that this is an easy task. While certain notions about love and romance may be very modern, the subject of love itself is quite ancient. One can go back quite a few centuries to find records of early human reflections on the meaning of love. Plato had a lot to say about it. In the Bible an entire book, Song of Songs is devoted to it. In every culture in the history of human civilization there have been people who have devoted a great deal of effort to the subject of love.

A study of the history of love reveals that every culture has its own way of defining love and its own way of influencing the development of expectations. That is to say that there is not one universal model, but various models of love that have been held up as models at different periods of human history. During the age of chivalry, for instance, unrequited love was the ideal. Someone has referred to this as love without sex, quite the opposite of our own age, in which sex without love has become a popular notion.

I am interested in late-twentieth-century America in this book. Our contemporary culture has its own ways of talking about, singing about, and portraying loving relationships. You may have not thought that American notions of love are particularly unique, but they are. The model or models of love being portrayed in America play a crucial role in creating the expectations that we have about our relationships. It goes like this: *models function in a culture to create expectations; expectations, in turn, determine whether people perceive themselves as happy or unhappy.*

People whose relationships reasonably fulfill their expectations perceive themselves as happy, while people whose relationships fall short of their expectations experience themselves as unhappy.

The truth is that the situation is even more complicated. I frequently start one of my workshops by asking people to write out their own definition of love. Then, at the end of the lecture, I ask them to look once more at their definition of love. Most of them are no longer happy with what they wrote; they discover that their definitions were too narrow or simplistic. They also discover that everyone in the group has a different definition. So within the broad cultural expectations that are created, we individually form our own unique definitions of love.

American notions of love and romance are not all that static. There was a time when we believed strongly that love and marriage belonged together and that you could not have one without the other. If you were in love, it should lead to marriage; and if you married, it should be because you were in love. That has clearly changed, since many couples now live together without being married. So you may now have love without marriage, but we still believe strongly that love should be present as the basis either for living together or for getting married. How does a culture communicate its models and definitions of love? In an oral culture, models of love are communicated through stories and songs handed down from generation to generation. In a literary culture, the models are communicated through essays and novels. In an electronic culture like ours, the models are communicated through movies, radio and television programs, songs, and the Internet.

Listen to the songs we sing in America. They are mostly about love. Look at the plots of the movies offered on any day of the week; they are about love and relationships. Check the weekly television offerings; many of them are about the agony and the ecstasy of love—love fulfilled, unfulfilled, spurned, rejected. I go to the movies and I watch the television programs. I see the same things you do, but I admit that I view them with a critical eye. I am looking for what kinds of models these movies and programs present for people in this culture.

Over the years I have come to the conclusion that there is a fairly consistent set of notions that are presented as to what love is and what love is not. Don't think that these notions are clearly spelled out because they are not. But they are there nevertheless, in the dialogues of the characters and even in the orchestral crescendos of the background music. Here is a summary of what I think people growing up in America learn about love.

Notion 1: Love Is Magical and Mysterious

The first and most powerful notion of all, perhaps, is that love belongs to a realm far removed from the everyday reality of utility bills, sick kids, and laundry soap. *Love belongs to a realm, best understood as magical and mysterious.* In other words, love belongs to a realm of mystery and magic, which are things we don't quite understand in the way we understand how to operate a computer or prepare a meatloaf.

You saw this at work in the movie *Sleepless in Seattle*. We are privy to the fact that when our hero met his first wife (now deceased), he "felt the magic" the minute he took her hand. From that day on, because of that magic, they knew they would be together. Our lonely hero despairs that the magic will never happen again. And then comes the moment when he helps the heroine out of the cab. As he takes her by the hand, the orchestra tells us that the magic has happened. We know the happy ending is not far away.

The problem for the rest of us is that no orchestra plays *forte* in any of the moments of our lives. We are stuck with trying to figure out if there can be "magic" in our relationship. How, indeed, will we know if this is love or not. Those who insist that love is mysterious and magical have an answer. *You'll just know!* Something inside you will tell you that this is love.

This very fundamental notion about love is completely false. Love does not belong to some intuitive realm of mystery and magic. It belongs to the realm of human experience in the same way that your senses of taste, touch, and hearing do. It is in the same class as the experiences you have in which you know you are enjoying yourself or you know you are having a lousy time.

Am I being unromantic? I don't think so. I'm as romantic as they come. I am not denying that, in the early stages of a relationship, when two people have just met, a very expansive, almost giddy kind of feeling comes over people. But the truth is that very measurable biological things happen in the human brain, chemical reactions that can be explained. When those things happen, we experience sudden surges of energy, a tremendous sense of well-being, and the capacity to talk with this person for hours.

There is also the phenomenon of attraction. Why is it that some people are more attractive to us than others? This actually has much to do with our first caregivers. As babies we began to associate being fed, changed, and cuddled with the shapes of the people doing those things. Over a period of time, a "template" was taking shape in our brains. Later in life, when we meet people with certain features that are imbedded in those old templates, features we associate with that early sense of well-being, we find ourselves being attracted. I would add that cultural definitions of what is handsome or beautiful also affect this process, but not as powerfully as do those templates which were formed when we were babies and young children.

The truth here is that love belongs not to a realm of magic and mystery, but to the realm of human experiences of taste, touch, and a sense of well being. You can know whether or not you love someone, or whether someone loves you, and you don't have to depend on intuition.

Notion 2: Love Is Outside Human Control

The second notion that is part of the American mystique of love is that this magical, mysterious phenomenon is basically outside of human control. It may sound a little crazy when I say it that way, and people would be inclined to argue with me about that, but listen to how we talk about love. The language is very revealing. The most popular way we talk about a relationship with someone new is to say that we are "falling in love," or "have fallen in love." The word *falling* is what strikes me. A *fall* is something that happens accidentally. Is that what we mean? Apparently, because we continue to say it that way.

Please note that "falling" is not something people do deliberately. We do not say, "I think I'll go out in the back yard this morning and fall." I know that there have been scam artists who have made a living out of "falling" into taxicabs or busses on the street, but those are most certainly not accidents. They are premeditated and deliberate; they are not real falls. A real fall is something that happens because we don't notice an obstacle. A real fall is an accident, something that we do not control. Since it was not intended, we are therefore not culpable. Our children don't intentionally go outside to fall and tear their clothes, they are the victims of accidents. The other driver did not intend to run his car into mine, he was distracted by something and failed to see the red light. It was an accident.

That is precisely how some people want to talk about love, as an accident over which they had no control. This dialogue might be heard on television: "I know it's wrong, but I can't help it. I just fell in love with you." My long-standing example of how "out of control" love can be is in a song Al Jolson sang that went "You made me love you. I didn't want to do it." I would agree that if someone could *make* me love them, then love *is* beyond human control. I have occasionally had a client who has told me that the reason he or she is coming in for counseling is so that I will make a spouse or lover love him or her again. I tell them that there is no way I can make anybody love anybody else.

You cannot be made to love. In fact, absolutely the opposite is true. Love is completely under human control. We do not "fall" in love with anybody. Instead, love is volitional, which is to say that we decide to love people and we also decide not to love people. We can decide to love people whom at one time we had decided not to love; and we can decide not to love people whom we had once decided to love.

Loving is a volitional act, or to put it more precisely, loving is a series of volitional acts. Let me illustrate. In an ongoing relationship with someone, in a marriage or a romance, there are an infinite number of exchanges, perhaps twenty or thirty per day. In these exchanges, my expectations either are being met or are frustrated, when they are not met. When my expectations, needs, and desires are met, I usually respond with the decision to love; that is, to return the investment in some way to my beloved. Only very immature or hopelessly narcissistic persons expect only to receive and never to give back mutually to a beloved. When, on the other hand, my needs, desires, and expectations are frequently denied or rejected, when a pattern of neglect or abandonment appears to be taking shape, I am likely to decide not to love.

In every relationship there are what I call "hinge experiences." A hinge is something that enables the door to turn, and a hinge experience is one on which a relationship begins to turn. Examples of hinge experiences are a woman discovering that her spouse has been involved in a shady business deal or a man discovering that his spouse has been lying about her activities. The discovery is sometimes sudden and dramatic, at other times it is a gradual awareness gained over a period of time. I do not mean to say that you must be in constant fear that whenever you fail your beloved the relationship is doomed. Or that you dare not say "no" for fear that the person will decide not to love you anymore. We are not that demanding or petty. That is why I used the word pattern above. If I show up an hour late some night, I don't expect that my spouse will terminate our marriage; but if a pattern develops in which I am consistently late, I know my spouse is going to get upset. And if other negative patterns also develop, there is every likelihood that my relationship may be at risk.

Sometimes a hinge experience is just one colossal, traumatic event like a man coming home and finding his spouse in bed with another man. More often the hinge experience is something that accumulates over several years, during which a particular hurt is experienced over and over again. The decision to love or not to love is made on such experiences, however, and because it may happen over long periods of time, people talk about "gradually falling out of love." The change is gradual, but people are not falling; it is a gradual process of deciding not to love.

Notion 3: Find Someone Who is "Right for You"

The third notion you learn about love as you grow up in America is that the secret to a happy, fulfilling, and enduring relationship is finding the person who is "right for you." In fact, the words used often suggest that someone must be "the right one," suggesting that, of all the hundreds of millions of people in the world, there is only one who is the right one for each of us and our task is to find that person. Think of that! This notion implies that the human family was created in matched pairs and that the incomprehensible task of each one for us is to find the one and only right one.

I would hope you would experience a great sense of relief to know that everything about that notion is untrue. The world was not created in matched male/female pairs. There is not just one person out there who is right for you. There are hundreds of thousands of persons out there who could be right for you.

I will admit, however, that the notion of two people not being right for each other is a nice way to let somebody down when you want to terminate a relationship. It's a lot better than saying something that causes someone to think they have some faults that are barriers to a relationship; but let's just keep it at that. It's a nice way to let someone down, not a description of reality.

I see two dangers for relationships if people actually believe that notion. The first danger is that it will be wrongly used as a rationale for absolving me and my partner for problems in our relationship. If I can interpret any conflict or lack of compatibility to our not being right for each other, I am never going to experience much of the potential depth that is possible in relationships. Except for instances of abuse, you don't cut and run at the first sign of having to really understand each other, forgive each other, and work out some differences. There is no such thing as a perfect relationship or a fit so perfect between two people that they never even have to work at it.

The second danger is that when I ask myself if someone is right for me, it means that my focus is on the wrong person. Let me illustrate. A young man came to see me once who was casually dating three different women. Tom thought that he was getting to the age where it was time to "settle down and get married." What brought him to see me? He said that people in his family had not done a good job of picking the right spouse. His parents were divorced, and he had three sisters, all divorced, one for the second time. You guessed it. He wanted to have some professional help in picking the woman who was right for him.

When I told him that there was no such person as the right one for him, he was greatly disappointed. I think he was a little suspicious of my competence as a counselor. I told him that not only was the notion of "the right one for me" not true, but as long as he approached the selection of a woman he would ask to marry him in that way, he had his focus going in the wrong direction. "As long as your focus is on the women, it is wrong. The focus should be on you," I told him. "Let's look at the three women you are already dating. By focusing on them, you end up comparing the relative attributes of these three. You can do plusses or minuses till you're blue in the face. What I want you to consider for a minute is that *you* are different when you are with woman A than you are with woman B or C. The important question is not which of these women is right for you. Any one or all three could be. The real question you should be asking yourself is, 'With which one of these women am I being what is right for me?'"

To ask this question is not selfish or selfcentered. It is indicative of a profound truth, that in a good and healthy relationship each person can be herself or himself. The question does not demand that I must try to be something or someone I am not. I don't have to suppress some part of me that I like. I don't have to be afraid to be me in order to be loved by you.

Gary came to me because he had just been dumped by a woman he had been going with for some time. She was a beautiful and vivacious woman. She had grown up in family invaded by alcohol abuse, and like many children who grow up in a family that felt out of control, as an adult she felt uncomfortable in any job or relationship in which she did not have a great deal of control. We spent some time going through the history of their relationship. When we started, Gary wanted me to help him come up with some strategy he could use to restart the relationship, but after just a couple of sessions, he confessed to me that he had just begun to realize how many things he liked to do he had given up for her. Now that he was alone again he had started adding some of the activities that gave him considerable satisfaction and pleasure back into his life. He realized how much of himself he had given up, how radically he had changed his life in order to conform to the things she wanted to do and the way she wanted to live. He also began to realize how much some of her little quirks irritated him, but that he had suppressed any conflict so as not to disturb the relationship.

Now I am not suggesting for a minute that we don't make minor to major adjustments in our lives when we get into a relationship. Compromise and adjustment are part of any relationship. I am really talking about the vital characteristics of who we are as persons, about our identity. We cannot be expected to give those up. I have always been a fairly permissive parent, actually a fairly permissive *person*, period. That's who I am. For the sake of a better relationship, I am willing to reign in my permissiveness a little, but I am not going to try to become Mr. Strict. I would be painfully uncomfortable in that role. I wouldn't be me.

Not being who you are, by the way, is why people with low self-esteem have such a difficult time in relationships. You have to like yourself before anyone else can like you. You need to be a person. You need to have an identity that you accept. It is also why people with low self-esteem are frequently attracted to people with above average self-esteem. It's as though they hope some of the high self-esteem will rub off on them. It won't.

So if finding Mr. or Ms. Right is not the secret to a happy relationship, what is? I am inclined to say that there is no secret at all. There is no magic bullet, no one thing, no simple formula by which anyone is guaranteed a fulfilling relationship. A good relationship takes hard work, but I do not want to associate "hard work" with something grueling or unpleasant. Exercise can also be hard work, but people who do it will tell you it can give you a real high. The work of loving can be just like that, hard work that gives you a real high.

If I were to make a true sentence using the words "secret" and "loving relationship," however, my sentence would be this: The secret to having a quality loving relationship is to work constantly at loving; and by *constantly* I mean all the time. I say that because, after forty years of listening to the stories of the histories of relationships, I have discovered that there was always a time when both people were really working at having a loving relationship—during courtship. When we are seeking to woo and win, we work at it. Apparently the notion is that, having won, we don't have to work at it anymore, or at least we don't have to work as hard as we did during courtship.

I am not implying that problems do not show up during courtship. Of course there are. By the way, we should pay careful attention to those problems because they are most likely to show up in the marriage later on. Most of the serious problems couples later identify in their marriage were clearly visible during courtship, even though they may have been less intense at that time. There is a notion in America that true love will conquer all. People make all kinds of promises that their jealousy, reckless driving, obsessive buying, or what have you will be given up after the wedding, but don't believe them. There is nothing about a twenty-to thirty-minute wedding ceremony that will make any of those character or behavior issues go away. Insist that the changes occur during the courtship instead of waiting until after the wedding.

If we do a good job of working at marriage during courtship, why doesn't that carry over into the marriage relationship? I have two answers for that question. The first is that most all human effort is goal-directed. We manage money carefully for two years to get the car paid off. We faithfully work at the lawn to eliminate the dandelions. Effort is expended in order to accomplish a particular goal. So what happens if you make "getting married" the goal? Simple, you expend the effort necessary to reach that goal. You work to get to the wedding, and when you reach the goal, the effort can be reduced or eliminated altogether. A couple who has worked hard to reach the goal of getting married now really need a new goal, but most people forget about that. We act as though, once we get to the wedding and the state of marriage exists, we have it made.

As a result, after reaching the goal of getting married, what happens is that many people turn quite consciously and deliberately to other goals. In America, that traditionally means acquiring the things that our culture tells us belong to the good life—a home, cars, an entertainment center. Since all of those things require money, both people put their noses to the grindstone so that the good life may be acquired; they may replace any relationship goals with career goals. Time and energy for the relationship takes second, then third place, it may eventually fall to the very bottom of the list.

The second reason the work of building a relationship does not carry over into marriage is thus one of distraction. We get so distracted by other priorities that the needs of the relationship suffer. And then comes the first child. This is a major event for any relationship, an enormous distraction from a relationship's dynamics. I do not imply anything against children, but while American family mythology correctly speaks highly of the positive benefit of children, there is also another side.

I discovered that other side in an important research project reported in a 1989 book entitled *The Birth Of The Family: An Empirical Inquiry*, by Jerry Lewis, a medical doctor. The focus of this project was to discover the affect the first pregnancy and birth of a first child has on the marriage of a couple. What they found is that a decline in marital quality begins with the onset of pregnancy and lasts for up to six months postpartum for females and up to eighteen months postpartum for males. In addition, the project found that if the relationship was of high quality before the pregnancy, it returned to that high quality. If it was already somewhat strained, the relationship slipped even lower on the scale of marital competence.

This was such a surprise for me that I scrapped the speech I had prepared to give at a breakfast for ministers and shared the stunning results of this research project. I suggested to them that we perhaps ought to take a look at the fact that most of us were spending a lot of time with couples in premarital education but virtually ignoring doing much with couples around their first pregnancy and birth of a child. Quite obviously, I do not think that children can be blamed for the failure of a relationship. Children, especially newborn children, demand a great deal of time and energy. They must have some of the very best care that we can give, but even with all the care they need, and with all the time it takes to give that care, I insist that a couple can still have a very high priority for their marriage. This will not happen automatically, of course. Couples may have to make some major changes, but the period of time in which infants demand twenty-four-hour care is not that long, perhaps three months at the most. Couples then can make the time to be together alone for dinner, a walk, a drive. By the time the children are age five or so, I do not think that it hurts children at all to discover that they come second and that their parents' marriage comes first. In forty years of listening to adults talk about growing up as children in their families, I have yet to hear anyone complain that his or her childhood was deficient because their parents put the marriage relationship first. On the contrary, children usually delight to see their parents sharing affection, solving problems, and being a happy married couple.

There is no magic bullet, no golden key, no simple formula for a happy lifelong relationship. We can have a happy, fulfilling relationship provided we are willing to work at it constantly in order to make it happen. This means refusing to be distracted by all the other demands of life, whether children, careers, or even disaster. It means making our relationship the top priority of life. The secret is not finding the right person, it is that we have to work constantly at loving.

Notion 4: The Need for Sexual Compatibility

The fourth notion in the American mystique about love is that the central key to the one who is right for you is sexual compatibility. "Don't you think that, when all is said and done, marriage relationships are made or broken in the bedroom?" I was asked that question at the end of a speech some years ago. Many people believe that, but I do not. That does not mean I don't believe what happens in the bedroom is important; of course it is. The sexual component of a relationship is extremely important and sexual compatibility is also very important.

What I am objecting to is the notion that sexual compatibility is the *key* to the person who is right for you. It simply is not true that the excitement of the kiss, the goosebumps of the caress, or the ecstasy of the orgasm tell you that you have found Mr. or Ms. Right.

The truth is that you can be sexually compatible with at least a million and a half people. I am writing these words the morning after an evening session with a group of senior high school girls, and I shared this truth with them last night. Their open-mouthed astonishment gave way to a questioning puzzled kind of look. I told them that, frankly, I wish that my statement was not true. Obviously, it is a dangerous truth, especially with the prevalence of sexually transmitted diseases and HIV. But I had to tell them the truth, and the truth is you can experience excitement, goosebumps, and orgasms with a great many people. As a result, simple sexual compatibility cannot be the key to finding the one who is right for you.

I most certainly am not suggesting that you conduct your own experiment with as many people as you can in order to test whether I am correct or not. Sex is too important to turn it into a game we play with many people. There are still people today who talk about something they call "recreational sex." They imagine, I suppose, that it is something like playing tennis with someone. It isn't. In being sexual with someone, there is a far more profound level of investment than there is in playing tennis. Your personhood, your identity, and everything you are as a person is involved; and aside from the risk of disease, you can be deeply hurt. I see in my practice a steady stream of people who have discovered too late that what they thought was "casual" or "recreational" sex is anything but casual.

I am not turning sex into something "serious" and "heavy" here. In a loving relationship, sex should be and is playful and fun. Like a lot of things we do that are fun, however, sexual behavior has its own internal rules and requirements. Playing games can be fun, but note that almost every game has its own rules, and if you ignore those rules the fun will soon disappear. Sexual behavior likewise has its own rules. For example, quality sexual fun involves the capacity to abandon yourself entirely to the playfulness of the sexual encounter. To totally abandon yourself to another in a sexual encounter requires trust, so one of the first rules about sex is that, over time, trust in and commitment to one another must be present or our body's sexual function just won't respond very well.

I know there is a big argument going on these days about sexual abstinence. I am happy that more and more of our high school young people are hearing that they don't have to become sexually active to be considered grown up. As I write today, I have just heard on the news that the incidence of high-school-age HIV infection is doubling every fourteen months. That's very scary, if it is accurate. There is nothing naïve or goody-two-shoes about "saving yourself for marriage" as folks used to say.

That used to be a much easier job when folks got married at seventeen or eighteen. It is a lot harder when people are postponing marriage into their late twenties or early thirties. My own recommendation, which applies to all ages, is that sexual relations ought to wait until there is a real commitment to the intention of permanence in the relationship. Even if you are middle aged and starting all over, it is still a good idea. Sex before commitment, even if you are sixty, is not a good idea.

Notice that my recommendation does not use the "M" word. This will raise objections from people who will accuse me, especially as a priest, of forsaking traditional and biblical standards of morality and suggesting that it is ok to have sex outside of marriage. My answer is that I have no objections to people who want to maintain their own sexual abstinence and limit sexual relations to the married state.

The world of the Bible was a far different world sexually than ours is. Most girls in the biblical world were married by the age of fourteen. Women were the property of men, and much of the sexual activity that was proscribed has that presupposition as its background. For a man to have sex with a woman outside of marriage involved the exploitation of property that belonged to her father or her husband. There simply was no situation in life in which a woman was not the sexual property of some man, but that is not the world we live in. And none of us wants to go back to that kind of world.

I am indebted to William Countryman, and his book *Dirt, Greed and Sex: Sexual Ethics in the New Testament and Their Implications for Today*, for this understanding about how the notion of sexual property has changed between the world of the Bible and our world. In today's world, my sexuality is my possession. It belongs to me, and yours belongs to you. I have a responsibility to myself to protect that which is mine. But my minimum demand, before I trust anyone with my sexual property, is that there be a commitment to me before I share what is mine with anyone.

I am unable to give proper credit for the following example, but the author or speaker, who was addressing the issue of at what point we could have sex suggested that we ask ourselves when in our relationship we would be prepared to share a checking account into which each of us would put all our money and trust it to the other. The answer to that question will tell you whether you protect your sexual property as well as your financial property. I pass on here what I think is a very good illustration of the problem.

Another important rule about sexuality is that it should be mutual. Marriage itself does not make any and all sexual behavior right. Sex is intended to be a mutual playing, a mutual sharing of pleasure. Something very dysfunctional happens when one partner only gives and the other only receives. Both should give and both should receive.

The really important point I am attempting to make with all of this talk about the relationship between sex and love is this: it is the quality of loving that is the key to sexual quality, not the other way around. I have sometimes worked with couples who are dealing with some severe obstacles to sexual compatibility, any one of a number of barriers to sexual pleasure. I have found that when these people truly love each other, as evidenced by their commitment to bring more pleasure and excitement to their relationship, their love sustains and motivates them. Again, their love is the key to sex, not the reverse.

Notion 5: Everyone Knows How to Love

The fifth notion that is a part of the American love mystique is that loving is something everyone knows how to do. Just think for a minute about how fundamental loving and being loved is to human well-being. Wanting to be loved shows up universally on lists of what people say they hope to experience in life. Given that everyone wants to be loved and to love in turn, it must be the case that a great deal of time and effort is devoted to teaching people how to give and how to receive this precious commodity, right? Wrong.

There are lots of books on love. Authors have written about love and its fundamental significance for human beings as far back as we can find any writing at all. Most all of the great thinkers of the past have devoted countless words to the subject. I think about all those great thinkers of the past when I sit down to write, and I wonder what makes me think I could possibly have anything to say that hasn't been said by hundreds before me.

Yet when I look at the education curriculum of the modern world, I have difficulty finding any sustained effort to teach people what they need to know in order to love another person, or how they might recognize when they themselves are being loved. I believe the reason for this puzzling absence is that there is an underlying assumption that either love cannot be taught or does not need to be taught. Both options of that assumption are wrong. People can be taught how to love. People need to be taught because we are not born with the knowledge of how to love. We are born with the potential to love, but only the potential, not the knowledge of how one goes about the task of loving another.

So where do we learn the strategies and techniques of loving? For most of us, the first place we learn is in the family into which we are born. Most of us are born into families in which we were wanted, treasured, and valued. We were nourished, cuddled, and encouraged. We were the object of someone's loving care and attention. And, in addition, as we grew we were witnesses to a relationship, the one modeled for us by father and mother. To the degree that the relationship between our parents was a good one, we got a good model of a loving relationship.

Not everyone grew up in such a home, however. Many many people grew up in homes in which the relationship modeled by their parents was horrible. There may constantly have been loud, angry words, and sometimes even physical abuse. Fathers or mothers may have engaged in addictive behaviors or become dysfunctional because of personality disorders or mental illness. Or the relationships may have been stable and enduring, but absent of much in the way of joy and feeling and happiness.

Growing up, we also saw other models, such as those models of love, romance, and family I talked about that are provided by movies and television programs. *Little House On the Prairie*, *The Waltons*, *Father Knows Best*, and *The Brady Bunch*, have given way to *Dharma and Greg*, *Friends*, *Step By Step*, *ER*, and *Seinfeld*. What all these popular shows have had in common is that they have dealt with the joys and disappointments, the successes and failures of relationships. We respond to these programs with laughter or pathos because they either portray the foibles we commit as human beings or reflect the experiences of our own lives. We have been learning from these programs even though we seldom think of ourselves as in a learning mode when watching a movie or sitcom on TV.

Through these movies and programs, as well as through the modern romance novels of the last three decades, we learn a lot of truth about love and relationships; but we also learn a lot of falsehood. And because we are often not in a critical mode when engrossed in a television program or reading a book, we have a difficult time separating truth from falsehood.

So where might we expect to learn how to separate the truth and falsehood about love? Whenever a society decides it is important for its people to learn something, that society includes it in the basic educational curriculum to which members of the society are exposed. The emphasis here is on the word basic. How to love ought not to be an elective. Everybody ought to be given a chance to learn this important skill early in life, certainly by the time we finish high school.

So is it in the curriculum? Not, as you are aware. If a student happens to be on the right track, he or she may touch on how to love in an introductory psychology (or sociology) class, and it frequently gets mentioned in some social studies courses. Many colleges and universities that require all students take a humanities course incorporate some of the authors who write about love, but we are not systematically and intentionally offering the children of America an opportunity to learn how to really love another human being. Children learn nothing about how you establish an intimate relationship with another person and how you maintain that intimacy over a period of time. If this is such a big problem, why has no one noticed it before? My answer is that the reason nobody noticed it before is because a major change in what people are expecting out of relationships has occured in the last century. Quality intimacy, or quality loving, is an ideal that has been around for a long time, but only in the last century has the expectation developed that this quality intimacy should characterize not only the initial stages of relationships, but should endure through the entire marriage.

My paternal grandparents had a very stable and enduring relationship. I would be very surprised if either of them ever even considered the possibility of divorce. There were plenty of times, I suspect, when they got angry at each other, even times when they raised their voices, though I never heard it. If I had asked them if they had a happy marriage, they would have answered in the affirmative. While neither of them was ever unhappy or upset for long, I know neither expected that they would experience throughout their married life what people today are expecting. I will admit that I expect more from my relationship with my wife after twenty years than Grandpa and Grandma expected out of their relationship. The reason nobody noticed the problem before is that it was not always a problem. Our expectations of our relationships have become more demanding. Some think too demanding.

One clue that we have been getting more demanding about our relationships is the high divorce rate in our society in recent decades. While there have been some fluctuations, that rate remains very high; and even if it were to maintain the present rate, it would be bad news. There are currently about one million, two hundred thousand divorces annually in the United States. In each of those divorces, an average of one child is involved. That means three million six hundred thousand people are directly involved in the pain and hurt of divorce every year. And I have not even counted the grandparents, aunts, and uncles.

This enormous problem has gotten the attention of the churches, many of whom have significantly improved their premarital education, and created marriage encounter and marriage enrichment opportunities for their members. But half the people in America do not go to church, and only a small fraction of those who do ever take advantage of the opportunities offered to improve relationships.

From time to time, the divorce rate has also gotten the attention of our legislators. Over the years, states have rewritten divorce statutes in an effort to respond humanely to the misery and unhappiness experienced in many relationships. One of the most humane of those responses, in my opinion, was the development of the so-called "no fault" divorce, although they could have given it a better name. I suggest "both fault," which is closer to the real truth. The purpose of this statute was to keep an already painful and ugly situation from getting worse by forcing people to charge one another with some kind of civil crime. Another purpose, frankly, was to put a stop to the wholesale commission of perjury in states where only one or two grounds for divorce were allowed. People routinely lied in order to qualify for one of the grounds.

Unfortunately, all around America these days states, including my own Iowa, are trying to change the divorce statutes and get rid of "no fault" statutes. According to many legislators, "no fault" divorce has made divorce too easy, so if we make it harder for people to divorce, they won't do so as often. I am very much in favor of taking constructive action to prevent so many divorces, but eliminating "no fault" divorce statutes will not accomplish that. It will, instead, increase the agony. It will create more separations. It will leave more women and children in limbo, abandoned by husbands and fathers without support.

The most constructive changes our state legislators could make are twofold. First they should mandate that couples who are divorcing and have children under the age of eighteen seek mediation and education and post-divorce strategies for parenting their children even though they are divorced. Children don't cause divorce, yet they often suffer the most severe consequences. They often must endure one parent bad-mouthing the other constantly. They are used as pawns in "get even" strategies by their parents. Mother denies visitation because the child support is late. Dad denies child support because he thinks his ex-wife is spending too much on clothes. The list goes on, but the sad fact is that, after a divorce, children continue to need both parents in their lives.

The second step legislators should take is to mandate more marriage and family-life education before issuing a marriage license. As a first step in that direction, we need a law in every state that requires a couple filing for a wedding license to provide a certificate of proof that they have had twelve hours of premarital education. There are plenty of qualified social workers and marriage counselors around who can advise the legislators on the content of such education. I would insist that at least three hours be devoted to the study of what loving is, what it is not, and how intimacy is both established and maintained in human relationships.

We already do something similar in every state in regard to licensing people to drive cars. We have drivers' education classes. Realistically, taking drivers' education does not guarantee that everyone will be a safe driver, but certainly no one doubts that we would have a lot more accidents if we did not continue to insist on this. I will not contend that taking classes in marriage and family life will eliminate divorce, but over time, I believe it would contribute to the lowering of divorce rates in our country.

In this consideration of what a loving relationship looks like, my point is that people have to learn how to love, and that simple truth needs to be acknowledged. Once we admit that truth, I am confident that we will devise ways to help people learn how to love. Notice, that I also framed the task as one of teaching people how to establish and maintain human intimacy. I did so because that intimacy is the issue today; it was not the issue a century ago.

As recently as the 1950s, much attention was focused on the mutual and complementary roles played in our culture by men and women, husbands and wives. It was taken for granted that the primary role for which men were responsible was to be a good provider. Men were to go outside the home to work, to earn the money it took to pay for a house, food, and clothing. Women were encouraged to play the primary role of emotional caretaker of the children and to be the homemaker. Those role expectations are still powerful in our culture. While there are, here and there, some househusbands who stay at home with the children while the wives are away from home earning a living, those situations are clearly in the minority.

In most cases, what one sees is two people who work full time while the children are taken to a day-care center, or have a baby sitter or nanny. Mother is still the one, most of the time, who stays home from work to care for a sick child, or misses part of a day at work to take a child to the doctor. Fathers are doing a little more these days, but Arlie Hochschild's study *The Second Shift: Working Parents and the Revolution at Home*, suggests that the "little more" they are doing is in the child-care arena rather than the homemaker arena. Today there are thus a lot of relationships in which women are working full time away from home and doing at least another part-time job at home.

Dividing up the tasks of child care and housekeeping is an important issue in relationships today, and finding more equitable ways to divide those tasks will certainly help relationships. When one person carries most of the burden of child care and housekeeping, there will be resentment.

One more word about learning to love. I do not believe that a short course taught in high school is all that one will need for life. Learning to love is really not like learning to drive a car or ride a bicycle. It is more like learning to be a good cook or a good carpenter or a good pianist. I have always liked Erich Fromm's book *The Art of Loving*. Its title alone defines what love is, an art. If you want to be a great cook, finish carpenter or concert pianist, you have to work at it over a long period of time. Great artists of any kind don't get there in a day or a month. They practice long hours, day in and day out. Loving is more like that. It is something about which there is always more to learn; new techniques, new recipes, new arpeggios to challenge us. But make no mistake, these skills have to be learned. If you don't learn *how* to love, you will never do a great job of loving.

Chapter Five
The Doing Part of Loving

The Human Needs Behind Love

Up to this point, I have been talking about loving as something that you do. Another good term to use is *invest*. Which implies that I place something of me or something that is mine in trust with something or someone else. A loving relationship is a relationship in which two people mutually invest themselves in each other for both the other's and their own well being. I indicated earlier, this is something that is done constantly; if loving is a kind of investing, it means that each continually invests in the other.

The next consideration, then, is to indicate just how and in what ways one invests in another in order to promote that person's well being. At the beginning of my counseling experience, in the setting of a parish ministry, I remember that when I heard people profess love for another, or when I heard them accuse the other of not loving, I was puzzled about how one could tell. It seemed obvious to me that people who professed love for another clearly thought they were engaging in some kind of behavior in order to make their loving intentions manifest. And it was just as clear that, when people declared that they were not being loved, there must have been some experience they

expected to have that was not happening for them. As a result, I started looking for what kinds of experiences people were expecting or felt were missing.

The word *love* is, after all, an abstract noun, which means that people can,
if they want to, load it up with various kinds of baggage. The question, then
becomes, in what ways people load the term. What kinds of objective behaviors are people looking for? I gradually came to see that loving someone was
not a matter of doing just one thing; behind the human experience of being
loved there were actually five different needs that were being met. When these
needs were being met, people felt they were being loved; but when one or
more was not being met over some period of time, people felt unloved. It
seemed to me as though each person carries around inside five buckets and in
order to feel loved, one needs to experience that these buckets are all being filled.

The bucket seems an appropraite analogy because people can understand
that you have to put something in a bucket to fill it. Using the analogy of a
bucket, I can also explain that sometimes the bucket is very small and sometimes it is very large. Filling a large bucket calls for more effort and time. The
image of a bucket developed over the years as I counseled both couples and
individuals; as I began to think about these needs, my brain created images of
buckets. The five buckets described here are attention, recognition, respect,
affection, and separateness.

Bucket 1: Attention

The first need, or bucket, as I have come to call it, was for attention. Human
beings experience attention as one of the ingredients of love. Parents discover
this early on. Children crave the attention of their parents, and once they
discover ways to get their parents' attention, they repeat those behaviors whenever they feel any lack of attention. As a minister calling on elderly in nursing
homes, I discovered the need for attention is not something that we outgrow.
The residents of these nursing homes invariably asked me to stay longer and
talk with them, because for long periods every day there was no one to listen
to them.

Getting attention is a way of being loved. Its most profound experience is that of being listened to. And I mean really listened to. In much human conversation, people don't really listen; they just wait for a chance to talk. They are not hearing what the other person is saying; they are planning their own response. Look in on an all too typical family-room scene in which she says to him, Harry we need to talk about whatever. "Uh-huh," he says while turning the page of his paper or clicking the remote to see what's on the next channel. By contrast, look in on the couple across the street. They sit across from each other in the family room with no paper or TV to distract them. They have constant eye contact as they talk about their issue. It's easy to tell where quality attention is going on and where it is missing.

When you give me your full attention, it tells me you are interested in what I have to say. It indicates that what I have to say is important to you and affirms that I am important to you. Refusing to be distracted, making eye contact, and giving thoughtful responses all show that a person is giving you quality attention.

In the first half of life, the awareness of this particular need is more important to women than to men. Men need attention as much as women do, but in my experience they don't complain about the lack of attention they get in their relationships with women. There are two reasons for this. First, men get good attention from women, so they have nothing to complain about. Second, men take a lot of their attention needs to their arenas of work and social relations.

Women, on the other hand, tend to judge the quality of loving they are getting from a man on the basis of the amount and quality of attention they get. Does he listen? Does he remember that she told him about something last week? Does he make eye contact? Does he give serious responses? That's what women are looking for.

This situation, however, changes with midlife, when this bucket becomes more important to men. It is still important to women, but it is no longer the sole basis on which a woman decides how well she is being loved. For men at midlife, the satisfactions in the career arena are beginning to decrease. Midlife men are beginning to shift their priority from their job to the family, or to some other intimate connection. Many men have been an absent presence in their families, and therefore they may experience some profound disappointments when they discover that, given that absence, family members have gotten along without Dad's input. As a result, Dad may discover he has trouble being listened to. He therefore takes a new need for her attention to his primary relationship with his spouse. Just like the woman in her thirties who wasn't listened to very well, the man in his fifties may decide that a quality of loving, as revealed in quality attention, is missing.

Bucket 2: Recognition

The second bucket I discovered I call recognition. Recognition is my experience that you notice my accomplishments and that you are proud of me for what I have accomplished. It is what your school-aged daughter expects to see in your eyes when she shows you the perfect score she got on the math test. It is what your little-leaguer son expects to see when he catches the fly ball that wins the game.

This is the bucket that is so important to men early in their relationships with women. In fact, it is on the basis of this need that men make a decision about the quality of loving they are getting from a woman. Men want to be heroes to their women, and they are deeply offended if they are treated more like zeroes than heroes.

As it was with the need for attention, so it is with recognition; a change occurs around midlife. During the first half of life, women make attention their priority need and men make recognition theirs; a midlife woman would like a lot more recognition, and a midlife man would like a lot more attention. This is just another example of the kind of balancing I talked about in chapter one. Remember, though, that we are talking about degrees of importance, not radical changes. Midlife women still want attention, and midlife men still want to be heroes with plenty of recognition; but the balancing of the two needs causes a shift in importance.

Ray is upset about his marriage relationship with Janet. When he came to see me, their third and last child had gone off to college a couple of months earlier. Ray is fifty-six; Janet fifty-four. Up until two years ago, Ray was on the road a lot, gone for a week at a time twice a month. Janet complained about his being gone, especially when the children were younger, because she felt that she was not getting much help from Ray with raising the children. Then Ray reached the point where he did not have to travel any more. He had become sick of being on the road all the time, and he has really enjoyed being at home every night. He has been looking forward to the empty nest with just him and Janet, so he is more than a little upset that Janet wants to begin attending a nearby college to take some courses she has developed an interest in over the years. She has even given some thought to becoming a teacher, something she was not interested in when she was in college. Now at the time when Ray believes he would enjoy spending the evening just visiting with Janet, she is doing homework.

On Janet's part, she is irritated that she had a lot of lonely evenings hassling with the kids while Ray was on the road. She got used to finding adult conversation outside the home. She resents Ray's inability to be proud of what she is accomplishing in school and to show any interest in her homework or the papers she is writing. He needs attention. She needs recognition.

Bucket 3: Respect

The third bucket that we all carry around is respect. Respect is the value that someone confers on me. It is very much like self-esteem, but self-esteem is the value I confer upon myself. Respect is the value that others confer on me by the way they treat me. The two are definitely related. It is difficult for a person to have self-esteem if he or she is constantly criticized; it is also true that people with low self-esteem are frequently attracted to critical or abusive people.

The most profound experience of respect is the experience of being treated like an equal. Therefore it is in the context of this need that I want to talk about equality as a necessary ingredient in a loving relationship. There are a great many times in the lives of all of us when we consciously or unconsciously get into games of one-upmanship with people. Most of us work in places where there is an organizational chart, and we had better know where we stand on that chart. In most work systems, power is vested in a relatively few individuals; and it follows that when people are dealing with power, real closeness or intimacy does not develop. Most of us have had experiences with the abuse of power. A new consciousness about use of power in the workplace has led to many lawsuits being filed against corporate powermongers who have used their power to sexually harass or exploit employees.

What people often do not recognize is that power can be detrimental to a good relationship in the same way that it can be abused in the corporate setting. Tom and Kathleen's story is a good illustration of what I am talking about. Tom is a partner in a top legal firm. Kathleen did not work outside the home when their children were small. Tom gave her a regular and generous allowance to handle household expenses, clothes, and entertainment for the children, and he took care of all the bills. When he wanted a new car, he simply went out and bought one. He made all the decisions about investments without consulting Kathleen. He did not even go over quarterly statements with her so that she could understand the investments he was making to give them a secure future. "I have never felt like an equal partner in the marriage," Kathleen says. She has no criticism of Tom's generous allowance, but he has more power in the relationship than she does and makes many decisions without even explaining them to her. Tom sees himself, on the other hand, as a benevolent provider and insists that Kathleen has never lacked for anything. This may be true, but whenever Kathleen does need something out of the ordinary, she must ask Tom, which makes her feel "less equal." After she started working full time and, as she puts it "earning my own money," she began to feel more equal. In America there is simply no denying that the person who controls the money has the power. The quickest way to create an inequality in a relationship is to turn the control of money over to one person.

Equality has to do with more than money, of course. It means that my feelings, interests, tastes, likes, and dislikes deserve as much consideration as yours. No more, but also no less. It means that we attempt to make all our decisions by consensus, not unilaterally. This is not always easy to do, especially in two-career families. In some careers, advancement sometimes demands moving from one part of the country to another. It is a difficult job to stay equal when what will advance one career is detrimental to another, but somehow the equality needs of each person must be balanced with the priority of the relationship itself.

Beyond the issue of equality, perhaps the most profound way in which respect is denied is through verbal, emotional, or physical abuse. You cannot abuse physically or emotionally someone you respect. How can you confer value on another by name calling, by running someone down, by battering? Or, for that matter, by just not taking someone into consideration? You confer value on someone by taking their time, effort, values, opinions, likes, and dislikes into consideration.

The need for respect becomes even more important at midlife because we all begin to do some serious assessments then of where we are and where we had hoped to be. We begin to compare some of our dreams and expectations with the reality of which expectations have been realized and which ones have not been met, and we have expectations not only for ourselves but also for our relationships.

When Jim and Christie got married, they both agreed to give the business Jim was starting their priority. It was a service business that depended for its success on Jim being available to do onsite work, so Christie agreed to give her time to the shop. The expectation was that, as soon as the business could afford it, perhaps in two to three years, Jim would hire some help and Christie could finish her education and move into a career in interior design. Three, five, and then ten years came and went, and there was always some reason why she could not pursue her goal. Resentment grew, because even though the business could afford it, Jim found a need to purchase new equipment or to move into a new area of service, and he needed Christie to handle the office chores. Christie stopped asking, but she did not stop resenting. She gradually lost respect for Jim since, from her perspective, he did not keep his word. And she found other times when he did not keep his word. Eventually she decided to leave the relationship.

This respect bucket is so important that I tell people that they will not be able to love anyone they do not respect. This is why it is so important not to lose the respect of your partner. It is also why it is important for you to tell your lover when he or she is involved in something that causes your respect to be shaken.

Bucket 4: Affection

The fourth bucket is affection. Poets have talked about "affectionate glances," but I stress that affection involves physical contact. *Affection* is a word that covers a large variety of experiences of contact, including but not limited to sexual relations themselves. Love is communicated through touching, fondling, caressing, hugging, and kissing. In my counseling practice, I have used a video which gives very clear instructions on caressing the body of another, an exercise that may involve overlooking the most erogenous zones of the body entirely. I used to be amazed at how many people seemed to ignore caressing the body of a lover.

Most of us by now have seen how new born infants are caressed by mothers. I watched on TV one night as a mother was filmed caressing her premature infant through the armholes of an incubator. The commentator insisted that there was clear evidence that human touch, at even this early age, had a very positive benefit for neurological development.

Many couples quite frankly live with a severe deprivation of affection. Most people know how important touching and caressing are as a prelude to sexual relations, but they should also know that touching, hugging, and caressing promote human well-being, whether sexual relations follow or not.

Walter and Alma experienced a lot of resentment and frustration in their relationship, and, as a result, a great deal of emotional distance developed between them. They hardly talked to each other a great deal of the time. I suggested two strategies for them to practice. In the first, they were instructed to use sentences that began with "I" instead of "you." This is because people feel less attacked when we communicate with "I" messages. The other strategy was to practice a light-touch kind of caressing, demonstrated for them in a video that they watched in my office. After two weeks of practicing those strategies on their own, the emotional distance between them began to close significantly. Walter told me later that the caressing he and Alma did was the most effective of the two strategies, and he credited that strategy with turning their marriage around.

We live in a world that has had to deal with a lot of inappropriate and unwanted touching, I know. We now teach our children the difference between good touch and bad touch. Surely every person has the right not to be touched if he or she does not want to, but the misuse of this great behavior is not an excuse to stop engaging in it altogether.

Certainly the need for affection does not diminish with age. Midlife men and women continue to need affection as much as younger persons. Men at midlife will begin to experience a sharper sexual decline than the typical midlife woman, there is nothing about the aging process alone that involves an end to a full sexual life of arousal and climax. It may take more touching and caressing for a man at midlife to get aroused than it did when he was twenty-five. There may also be a decline in libido. Some men can become very anxious about all of this, and you can imagine what kind of effect anxiety will have both on arousal and performance. I suggest that midlife men talk with their partners about any changes in their libido or arousal. A woman who is used to a man being aroused without her having to do anything may simply need to be told that that is no longer the case. It does not mean he loves her any less. It does not mean that she is any less sexually attractive to him. It is just that his sexual response system is moving a little differently.

Any difficulty that persists for a male should, of course, send him to his friendly doctor. When there is a serious problem, it is usually the result of some sickness or severe stress in some arena of a man's life. Jonathan came to see me because, at the age of forty-eight, he was having difficulty achieving an erection. Jonathan had experienced one preadolescent experience of sexual abuse, and he wondered if that could have something to do with his problem. His spouse thought it had more to do with stress created by a severe conflict he was having with their adolescent son. She also wondered if she simply did not turn him on any more. I persuaded Jonathan to see a urologist, which he did. Much to Jonathan's surprise the urologist found a blocked artery in his groin. Needless to say, without enough blood a man is not going to have an erection. Surgery corrected Jonathan's problem. I routinely refer to the medical profession for problems such as this because if something is found, it is the easiest probable cause to eliminate. I could have counseled with Jonathan for several weeks, if not months, before sending him to a doctor, and he would have spent a lot of money on counseling needlessly.

I believe that the first thing anyone should do when experiencing problems with the sexual response cycle is to suspect something physical. About three out of five medications given to treat high blood pressure may cause sexual arousal problems for males. So will some antidepression medications. There are two significant reasons that midlife and older persons do not have satisfying sexual lives. The first, sadly, is that there is no available partner. The second is that there is a disease process which prevents it. The good news is that affection is not just for the young. It is an important need for the middle aged and for the elderly, too. Affection is a major contributor to well-being at any time in our lives, from infancy to old age.

Bucket 5: Separateness

The fifth bucket of need that we carry inside ourselves is one I call separateness. Years ago I called it "privacy," but that suggested something that was secret, and secrets are not good for relationships or for family systems. Then I called it "individuality." It was in the course of reading M. Scott Peck's book, *The Road Less Traveled*, that I found the word I had been looking for all along, *separateness.* As strange as it may sound, one of the ways that you love some-one is to honor their separateness. Each one of us is an absolutely unique creation. There has never been anyone exactly like us before, and there never will be anyone exactly like us in the future. (Even cloning will not change that.) Each of us has our own unique history, personality characteristics, dreams, fantasies, expectations, and goals for life; each of us is under an obli-gation to differentiate ourselves from our families and from everyone else. We also want to connect to others, but in ways that will not interfere with our self-differentiation.

I insist, in fact, that people who are not well self-differentiated have great difficulty with connecting in healthy ways with others. People with low levels of self-differentiation live in a world of feeling and emotion. They must de-vote almost all of their energy to finding someone to love them, and they form the kind of relationships that are characterized by the term *codependent.* As I write these words, there is a popular song out that is sung by the very young new country-western star, LeeAnne Rimes. "How Can I Live Without You?" the song asks. My answer is that you should be able to do that quite well.

I am not minimizing the pain of separation and death—those are trau-matic experiences that need to be grieved and recovered from but no emo-tionally healthy person places their only reason for living in or on someone else. This is why extremely needy people do not do well in relationships. They have yet to develop as persons. They have too desperate a need for others. Often, when they do make some connection with another person, they behave emotionally the way a drowning swimmer behaves when the lifeguard comes to rescue. They cling so desperately and so frantically that they threaten both lives.

I would argue that, unless you have a life of your own, you have nothing to offer in a relationship with someone else. I like to use the example of an orbit. Each of us needs our own independent orbit. Two people in a loving relation-ship must arrange their individual orbits so that they overlap. There are still two distinct orbits, but in the overlapping they create some time when they are together and some time when they are apart. There is shared space and private space, but not secret space. How much the orbits overlap depends on the needs of the two persons. It may also depend on where they are in the history of the relationship.

Orbits can be arranged so that they do not even overlap, but that is not much of a relationship. The two persons may live in the same house, but they do not share much with each other. At the opposite end is the "codependent" relationship. The way I draw that is to show one orbit that always stays inside the other one, which is also not a healthy relationship. The people in both of these orbit arrangements are vulnerable to an affair. In the first, with two orbits that do not overlap, that is obvious. Since both are quite alone and since there is a powerful human urge to be connected to others, either one is vulnerable. In the arrangement with one orbit inside the other, the one whose orbit is on the outside is usually the more vulnerable. This is because the one whose orbit is on the outside usually has the power. The one on the inside has traded away power for security. Both, however, are living with an illusion.

As you go from courtship to early marriage, to marriage with children, to marriage with adolescents, to midlife, and to old age, you and your partner's orbits may overlap more or less. In courtship there is a maximum of overlap, and this probably returns after retirement. Midlife is when the process of adjusting the orbits begins to move toward more overlap as the children go out into the world on their own and as outside demands become less important. It is also at midlife that the absence of a differentiated self becomes particularly critical, because the one with the higher differentiation feels like he or she is really carrying the responsibility of supporting the other emotionally. The relationship is very uneven and lacks mutuality. There is no taking turns; no sharing of the emotional burden when one person carries most of it for the other. People at midlife sometimes talk about feeling that they are raising an additional child, which is the result of one person developing and growing and the other not.

Honoring the separateness of a partner is always important, but especially so at midlife. It is also trickiest at midlife. The reason that it is so important and yet tricky is that midlife is the time when a lot of people want to change their orbits. Newspapers and local news programs carry these stories all the time. Here is the successful banker who, after thirty years in the banking business, opens up a new coffee and muffin shop downtown, where the little ice cream shop used to be. Here is a story about a successful lawyer who is giving up his plush law office to go to a seminary and become a minister at less than one third his former salary. Or here again the story of a woman who has raised three children alone after her husband's death who has decided to go into politics and is running for a seat on the city council.

For the great majority of people, their orbit transformations are less dramatic, but it is still the same phenomenon. The man who has never enjoyed dancing suddenly tells his wife that they should take dancing lessons. The shy lady everybody knew and liked surprises all her friends by getting involved in the community theater. The high school dropout signs up for accounting classes at the community college. The "steak and potatoes" guy explores vegetarianism. The loud and intimidating man suddenly mellows out. These changes can make honoring the separateness of your beloved so difficult, because what you may have to honor is something you have never seen before.

We have established that loving is something we decide to do. It is neither mysterious nor magical, nor is it an accident we "fall" into. When we decide to love, we enter into a relationship with our beloved in which we devote ourselves to filling the need buckets of the beloved and in response, the beloved fills our need buckets. This is done by investing in each other in specific ways so that our needs for attention, recognition, respect, and affection are filled and our need for separateness is honored. The secret to a successful and happy relationship is for two people to work constantly at this mutual bucket filling.

You do not have to be in the dark about whether you are being well loved or not. By checking out your five buckets, your experiences will tell you. And if you wonder whether you want to love someone or not, you only need to contemplate the enormous satisfaction, or lack thereof, of filling that person's buckets.

Tasks for Filling Needs

In addition to being aware of these five needs buckets, we must develop the ability to perform five "tasks." These tasks—being sensitive, extending one-self to invest, holding one's buckets out, telling and asking, and repairing one's buckets—will allow us to do a good job of bucket filling.

Task 1: Being Sensitive

The first of these is the task of being sensitive. We need to improve our sensitivity to one another, because we are not equipped with anything like the Doppler radar that the weather forecasters use to tell us exactly when the next storm will hit our little community. The task of reading another person's signs is also complex, but not impossible. Once you are committed to loving your beloved and you are together, the question is which of her or his buckets are the most in need of filling? How much should you put in? Is the greatest need right now for attention, or is it affection? Commitment is vital, but more is needed. The will to love must be harnessed to the ability to figure out, that is, to be sensitive to, which need you should respond to, and with how much.

Over time, people can actually get to be pretty good at reading the signs. That certain sigh means such and such, as does that way of slumping in the chair. The way she says, "Yeah, I suppose so," means she doesn't like something very much. That funny grin means something. Until you have been with someone for twenty years, you may have to ask, which is OK. You may ask, "What could I do that would help you the most right now? Would you prefer I just sit here by you, or would you like to talk about it? Would a hug help? When you say 'yeah, I suppose so,' in that tone of voice, you really mean you don't like it very much, don't you?" Statements like, "You seem down tonight" and "You seem bothered about something," or questions such as, "Do you have a headache?" tell our partners that we are picking up some signals and we want to check them out to see what they mean. It is truly rude and very unsympathetic to ignore obvious signs of distress.

The particular ability I am talking about here is empathy, the ability to feel with another. Very often, our partners are not asking us to solve their problems as much as they are asking us just to be there with them and to listen with empathy, as opposed to disinterest. A couple who attended one of my workshops wrote me a letter to thank me for the things they learned about loving. They also told me that, on the way home from the workshop, they stopped at a store to buy two sets of five buckets, one green, and one red. They labeled each set with the five needs I had talked about, and then they agreed that each of them would place the buckets in the order of her or his needs each day. (They might have to change the order more than once a day!) I have no objection to any strategy such as this that works to improve the quality of loving in a relationship, but one might hope that they would become good enough at reading each other that they would not have to look first at the mantle or the coffee table to know how much to put in what bucket.

Task 2: Extending Yourself

The second task is that of extending yourself to invest at the point of need. The first skill is necessary to determine the where the need is; skill number two is learning how to extend oneself to fill that need. Something has to be done that fills the empty bucket. I realize this may sound so obvious that you wonder why I even bother to mention it, but I insist that it is not obvious at all in real life. It is not true that anything you do will fill the bucket. Watch and listen carefully to television commercials and ads in newspapers. What do they suggest men should do to prove the genuineness of their love to a woman? They suggest buying a gift, and diamonds say it best. Yet, I daresay there are hundreds of thousands of women out there who would trade their gifts, including the diamonds, for more attention or respect. And how can women most effectively prove their love to a man? Be sexy is the message American women get. Again, there are hundreds of thousands of men who would trade some of that sexiness for recognition or for the honoring of some of their separateness.

One cannot assume that doing anything will fill the bucket. You may intend for it to do that, but intentions, as sincere as they may be, do not guarantee that the person with the empty bucket experiences the satisfaction we intended. Marty used to travel a lot, and, after several years of being on the road, his wife, Sue, used to dread being alone for a week at a time. Marty knew about her dread of his being gone, so when a trip was coming up he would present her with a gift certificate so that she could go shopping while he was out of town. Sue truly appreciated his generosity, but it did nothing to address the loneliness she felt. I suggested that Marty might consider inviting Sue to join him in the middle of the week for a couple days. Doing something like that would address the need directly.

Think of this task as giving us all a chance to use our creativity. The more creative we get, the more our partners appreciate the effort we are expending; and frankly, it is fun to figure out new ways to address the needs of one's beloved. There is more than one way to give attention, or recognition, or respect, or affection; there is more than one way to honor the separateness of another. In loving relationships, people are always looking for different ways to fill each other's needs. This means that love is work, but it can be work that is fun to do.

Task 3: Hold Out Your Buckets

The third skill we must learn is to hold our buckets out to our beloved. Loving involves the mutuality of meeting another's needs and expecting another to meet ours. If that is to happen, then you must extend yourself to fill the buckets of your beloved, and you must take the risk of holding your own buckets out. Some people are surprised to discover that the tasks of loving involve risk, but they always do. The nature of that risk here is that when you hold your buckets out to someone, they will be ignored. Rejection! Nothing hurts worse in all the world than to want someone to love you and to discover that they refuse. You are left standing there looking like a fool; and even worse, with empty buckets. Empty buckets hurt enough; rejected buckets hurt even more. In fact it feels like your buckets have been kicked instead of filled.

Almost everyone has experienced the pain of rejection. It happens a lot in the beginning. I have had a client as young as sixteen who was in absolute despair because he was rejected by the girl he wanted so much to love him. He took a whole bottle of acetaminophen after writing a note in which he said he wanted to die "because it was too difficult to find love in this world." You may think, as I did, that giving up on love at sixteen is a little foolish, but surely we are all acquainted with the kind of pain that he felt. There is no deeper emotional pain than that of being rejected by someone.

I have had many clients who, after a failed relationship, ask me how they can protect themselves against the pain of rejection. They want to begin to date again, but in a way in which they will not have to risk getting hurt. I tell them that there is no way to love or to be loved that does not involve the risk of being hurt. You cannot hold your buckets out and protect them at the same time. Building any kind of armor around yourself to keep from feeling pain only makes it impossible for someone to love you. The thicker the armor, the lonelier you feel.

However, you can be careful in relationships. I would not advise starting a relationship with anyone by trusting naively everything that is said. You do not have to make yourself completely vulnerable within the first week of the relationship. Be patient. Take your time. I would advise being particularly cautious if you do not perceive your partner doing the same thing. I know of people who have moved in together after the third date, which is clearly foolish. In the late adolescent to young adult stage of development, it takes a good year to get to know someone. The older you are, and the more experiences you have with people, the less time it takes to tell when someone is not who they say they are. Even in midlife, it takes four to six months to get to know someone really well.

I advise people that at the beginning of a relationship, it is a good idea to take your cue from the other person. Determine how much investment is being made by the other, then match it with your own. It is pretty easy to tell the degree of commitment someone has in a relationship with you. If you keep the five buckets in mind, you will soon know how much of a priority she or he is giving to the relationship. Then you can match that commitment. I know you cannot exactly quantify things like "commitment" and "priority," but you know when you are putting a lot more into the relationship than someone else is and when you discover that you should pull back until you know what is going on. And if you are really confused and unable to figure out what is going on, I suggest asking.

I believe that the temptation to get involved too deeply and too quickly is even stronger when we not only have been rejected, but rejected for someone else. We feel like we have been traded for someone younger, richer, thinner, more handsome, or whatever, and we want to prove our value. We need to know that we are still lovable. This was the situation with Virginia. She was overwhelmed when she found out that her husband was involved with another woman, twelve years younger than she. She immediately went on a dangerous diet, bought some new clothes, and began dating within two weeks of filing divorce action. Over the next six weeks, she had sexual encounters with three different men. She came for counseling because she realized that this behavior looked bizarre to her teenage daughter, and she was fairly disgusted with her behavior, too. Virginia had had a poor relationship with her own father. She felt that he had favored her older sister and that she could never impress her father. She remembers her father referring to her sister as "my beautiful one." "I guess I was the one that wasn't beautiful," she said. Her husband's rejection of her for a younger and more beautiful woman had re-opened what was an old wound.

Task 4: Tell and Ask

The fourth task that needs to be performed in a loving relationship is the task of telling and asking. This particular task is often very easy in the beginning of the relationship, at least the telling is. It is exhilarating to tell the other person about me and listen to her as she tells me about herself. The telling comes easy. People who talk to me about the history of their relationship often remember how much they used to talk. One of the answers that I often hear when I ask what originally attracted someone so much to a partner is that he or she was so easy to talk to. People remember talking till 3:00 A.M. and wondering where the time went. The truth is, however, that they were talking about a lot fairly superficial stuff: food, music, movies, hobbies, and so on, not particularly heavy subjects. It sometimes takes several dates before we start talking about the deeper things. But compared to other times in a relationship, courtship stands out as a time when people are often much more communicative. One reason we tell and ask more freely in the beginning of a relationship is thus because we can start out with some fairly superficial information.

The second reason we tell and ask more early on in a relationship is that we are a little braver and willing to take more risks. We don't have much invested yet, and we can't be hurt as much if we don't have much invested. So what happens to that bravery or that willingness to risk? It decreases after the relationship becomes committed or it moves into marriage, and the reason it does is because a new reality appears: the distribution of power and control in the relationship. At this point we learn that anything we say may be used against us, or that being too open will subject us to criticism and negative judgments, so we begin to keep things to ourselves that could give our partners any advantage in the struggle for power. We become secretive, which is a strange contradiction. You would think that in a well-established loving relationship we would trust more, and we should, but this means we need to work at making our relationships more trusting.

Bob thought he had a trusting relationship with Sue, and in a very intimate moment he told her some things about himself that he had never shared with anyone. Within two weeks, the whole matter got back to him because Sue shared it with a female friend, who shared it with her husband, who was also a good friend of Bob's. From that moment on Bob, believed that he could no longer trust Sue with anything deeply revealing about himself. I counsel couples to imagine that they are like priests in a confessional who cannot tell anyone else, no matter what is revealed.

This is a good time to discuss secrets. Edwin Friedman, in *Generation To Generation: Family Process in Church and Synagogue*, writes that secrets in personal and family relationships act like plaque in the arteries of the human body. Secrets plug up the lines of communication, and they plug them up for all communication, not just communication about the secret itself. The more secrets that people keep from one another, then, the poorer any communication gets to be. Jack has been married previously and has two children by that marriage, a son, age eight, and a daughter, age six. He is now living with Kimberly, who has also been married before and has one son by that marriage. They are planning to be married in the near future. Kimberly, however, feels that Jack's children get a higher priority than she does. He is supposed to have visitation with his children one night each week and every other weekend. It irritates her that Jack goes out of his way to accommodate his ex-wife when she wants extra time away on her own by picking up the children at other times. Knowing how much his making extra time for his children irritates Kimberly, Jack has suggested to his ex-wife that she call him at work rather than at home, so that he can make arrangements without having to endure Kimberly's dirty looks. He often sees the children for an extra hour and keeps it a secret from Kimberly. Their communication, as a result, is very dysfunctional at the present time. In fact, their moving on into the marriage is now threatened by the communication problem. They have difficulty talking about almost everything, and Jack finds that he is not telling Kimberly about things that have no relationship to the children at all.

One rationale I always hear as to why one does not tell the other is because he or she wants to protect the other from being upset. I strongly urge against this kind of protection. In a healthy relationship involving two mature persons, neither should have the responsibility of protecting the other. It implies that there is something fragile about the other; it implies that one has a caretaking responsibility. Emotionally healthy people do not need caretakers unless they are ill or have some disability, and even people who are to some degree disabled should be encouraged as much as they can to do for themselves. When one party protects the other from information that may be upsetting it keeps that person in an inferior position. Pretty soon one party is behaving like a parent, and the other is treated like a child. When that kind of dynamic takes over in a relationship, quality love and intimacy begin to decline. In any relationship in which a pattern develops where one person always protects the other, the long term outcome is bad.

I have discovered that, over time, the one doing the protecting gets tired of doing that protecting. It takes more energy, but most of all it demands that the protector take more responsibility. Kirk had a problem with alcohol. He didn't drink on the job, but started immediately at quitting time. He would get home late, and then frequently drink some more. Jan had nagged at him to stop for years, but he insisted that work was stressful and that drinking was the only thing he could do to relax. He angrily told her that if it were not so stressful at home, too, he might not have to drink so much there. So Jan set about to keep Kirk from getting stressed at home. She didn't tell him about the bills she did not have enough money to pay. She didn't tell him about the problems one of the kids was having in school. She didn't tell him how much money it took to get the kids registered in school. For ten years she "protected" Kirk from anything unpleasant at home. Of course, this protection did not influence his drinking pattern at all. The outcome was that after ten years of protecting Kirk, Jan got sick and tired of it. She felt overburdened with responsibility because she had to shoulder it all alone. In my experience, this is what happens to all protectors. They get stressed themselves. They get resentful about bearing the burden alone, and sooner or later that growing resentment brings about an explosion, frequently one that results in terminating the marriage itself. It is appropriate to protect children, but we expect adults to be capable of sharing all the burdens of raising children and taking care of a home.

The other long-term consequence of a protector/protectee relationship is that one being protected invariably begins to perceive the protector as a persecutor. And so it was with Kirk and Jan. Kirk did not see Jan's protective behavior as benevolent at all. He saw it as keeping things from him; and then he wondered what else she wasn't telling him. He was sure she was spending money on things he would not approve. He wondered where the money came from that purchased her new coat. As far as he was concerned, all of the behavior that she intended to be protective had made his life worse. I would add that such is the perception of most people who are protected, not just those with a drinking problem.

My final comment on protective withholding is that I believe that the person who claims to be protecting the other is most often protecting him-or herself. We don't want to deal with the anger or conflict that will ensue, so if we can keep the other from finding out, we won't have to deal with another argument. Having a whole bag full of things you cannot talk about with your partner is an indicator of a serious problem; you both need to get to a counselor to identify what you need to do to change the dynamics of your relationship.

In a healthy relationship, both persons are able to ask for what they need and to tell the other what is going on in his or her life. One of the exercises I use with couples who have not had very good communication for a long time is to send each of them home with a sheet of paper with the beginning of a different sentence on each side. At the top of one side, the sentence begins, "Three things I wish you would do for me next week are:" On the other side, the sentence begins, "Three things I would like to do for you next week are:" They are each to fill in the blanks with specific objective behaviors. I tell them there are only two rules. The first is that you may not ask for something you know your beloved absolutely does not like to do. That's unfair. The second is that what you ask for must be specific and objective, not something subjective. "Be more understanding" is too subjective. "Turn off the TV for twenty minutes and talk to me about what is happening in your life" is a lot more objective. Each of them is obligated to fulfill the request of the partner and to follow through with what each promised to do for the other. A lot of couples tell me that when I gave them that assignment they thought it was pretty hokey, but they were surprised at how it improved their communication. It is important to learn to ask for what you want and to offer what you would like to share with your beloved. It is one of the tasks of loving.

The task of asking for what you want and telling what you have to offer is especially important at midlife, because what you want and what you have to offer may be quite different than earlier in your relationship. I cannot count the number of times I have listened to a midlife couple in counseling say something like, "I know I used to like that rice dish, but about five years ago I stopped liking it. I never had the heart to tell you." Or, "I know I used to like it when you were gone for a few days, but I stopped enjoying it a long time ago, and I resent you thinking that things would always be the way they were." Midlife is a time to bring it all up again and see whether our perceptions of each other are still valid.

Task 5: Repair Your Buckets
The fifth task which we need to do is the task of repairing our internal buckets. We are born with the five buckets I have described here—attention, recognition, respect, affection, and separateness—and we have those buckets all our lives, even when we live to be one hundred. None of us ever makes it from childhood to adulthood with all of our buckets in perfect condition, however. Between birth and adulthood our buckets are damaged. They have holes punched in them, some small, some large. Sometimes the damage is so severe that the whole bottom gets knocked out of the bucket. You cannot fill a bucket with a hole in it, and if the hole is large, whatever you put into it will run out as fast as you attempt to fill it.

How did our buckets get so damaged? The simple answer is that they got damaged because none of us had perfect parents. The parenting we received left something to be desired. I do not mean to suggest for one minute that most people had malicious parents who deliberately parented their children in ways to harm them. There are some parents who are severely incompetent, but fortunately they are in the minority. Most parents indeed love their children and intend to do the best job of parenting they can, but every generation has its own notions as to what constitutes good parenting. Sometimes the parenting strategies practiced by one generation are contrary to what will produce happy children who can function well in relationships when they become adults. In the 1930s in America it was not considered good parenting to give lots of cuddling and affection to your baby. Benjamin Spock, Bruno Bettelheim and other doctors then taught a very different kind of parenting. A trip to the woodshed was once considered good parenting; now it is more likely to be considered abusive. I am not trying to get parents off the hook. I merely want to affirm that most of our parents did the best job they knew how as they parented us. Often, what was lacking in their parenting was due to the way they in turn were parented.

Lori, a first child, grew up in a family where she seemed to never be able to get the attention and affection of her father. He was a cold and distant kind of man, and was himself an orphan, abandoned by his father after his mother's death. He seemed to be only critical of Lori. Lori found herself attracted to older men while in high school, and much to the disapproval of her parents, she was dating college age men in her junior year. By the time I met her, Lori was in her late thirties and had already had affairs with two of her doctors. Clearly, Lori was engaged in a pattern of behaviors that revealed her attention and affection buckets had the bottoms knocked out of them. In some of the family-of-origin work we did, we were able to get her father to cooperate. He acknowledged his emotional distance from his daughter, and they began working on a much closer relationship, one that helped Lori to repair the buckets which were damaged.

A very helpful explanation of what I am talking about is found in the book *Getting the Love You Want* by Harville Hendrix. As Hendrix explains, in our adult love relationships, it is as though we try to reset the stage with the same emotional realities that were there in our childhood relationships with our parents; then we can replay the action, only this time have a different ending. Unfortunately, the ending is often just the same. So Lori, who could be very seductive, found herself in relationships with older men, but men who were just as unavailable to her emotionally as her father was. She kept getting hurt all over again.

Brian came into counseling to get help with his relationships with women. He was married to Beth for six years and has a son, age four. Brian admits he had a drug problem while married to Beth. Beth used drugs too, but she stopped after the second year of marriage. Brian went through drug treatment about eighteen months before coming to me. He now has a relationship with Bernita who lives several hours away, so they see each other mostly on weekends. He experiences a lot of anxiety when they are apart, but a considerable amount when they are together also. His first wife left him for another man, and he confesses that he is constantly afraid that this woman, Bernita, will also leave him. When it is her turn to drive to his apartment, he begins to experience an uncomfortable anxiety when she is only five minutes late. When she was several hours late on a recent weekend, he said it was unbearable. He was sure that she had found another man and would not be coming.

I was prepared to send Brian to his doctor to determine whether or not he was suffering from an anxiety disorder, but postponed that when we got into the family-of-origin work-up. Brian lost both of his parents before the age of six, and he and an older sister were raised in an adoptive family. His adoptive father was a depressed man with an alcohol problem. He and his adoptive mother never connected emotionally; he has a better relationship with her now as an adult than he did as a six-year-old boy. Brian suffers from an "orphan syndrome." His mother did not die deliberately, obviously, but to a six-year-old abandonment is abandonment, regardless of the cause. Now I understand even more why he lives with the feeling that Bernita may give up on the relationship and find another man. The significant women in Brian's early life have all abandoned him, and so have the significant men. Brian is in the process of learning to trust that someone in whom he invests love will not abandon him.

The good news is that damaged buckets can be repaired. Sometimes they can be repaired rather quickly when the parents or surrogate parents are still around. It is more difficult if the significant early caretakers are deceased. Calvin, a midlife man, had been married twice and was currently living with a woman with two teenage daughters. That is, he was surrounded by women. His occasional bouts of anger were more than Roberta, his partner, could handle, and she demanded that he get counseling or move out of the home. Calvin was ready to believe that there was something lacking in the way he related to women. He admitted that his first two marriages had ended because the women could not stand his temper, although he had never been physically abusive. He had a good relationship with Roberta's two daughters, born in her previous marriage. However, he did feel jealous of the attention and affection the daughters got from their mother. He claimed that his anger was justified because the daughters came before him on Roberta's priority list. You can guess what the family-of-origin workup brought to the surface. Calvin belonged to that minority of persons who have had maliciously dysfunctional parents. Both his father and mother were alcoholics. Calvin was a second child who was physically and sexually abused by his alcoholic mother. As soon as he could get away from home, he did; but he admitted that he had never really vented his anger at his mother. He decided to attend her funeral, he said, just to make sure she was really dead. I helped Calvin through a series of exercises in which he vented some of that anger. One of the exercises involved writing a letter to his mother in which he expressed his anger and then reading the letter to her at her grave. By the end of the series of exercises, Calvin and Roberta were able to recommit to their relationship, and in fact were making plans to get married.

As I said above, the good news is that buckets can be repaired. The bad news is that you have to repair your own buckets. No one else can repair them for you. Somehow we think if we can just find someone to love us, often unconditionally, all of our broken buckets could be fixed. But that is not the case. Think of it this way: with holes in your buckets, it is next to impossible for someone to love you, no matter how caring and loving that someone is. To love you, they have to fill your five buckets; but if the buckets have holes in them, or worse, the bottom is out, you can't be loved. Whatever people do will never be enough, because what is put in at the top of the bucket leaks out the bottom. So you must fix your own buckets and I must fix mine.

Another author who has focused on this problem is John Bradshaw, who calls it "healing your inner child." He has written about it in a book called *Homecoming*, which I heartily recommend to those who have buckets in need of repair.

～

In this chapter, we have seen that loving is something we each must take an active part in. We love someone by investing ourselves in them in order to fill their needs for attention, recognition, respect, and affection and for having their separateness honored. The tasks we need to practice in order to do this are developing our capacity to be sensitive, investing so as to fill their buckets, holding our own buckets out to them, learning to ask for what we want and to tell what we want to offer about ourselves, and finally, repairing our own buckets so that we can actually experience being loved when someone is investing in us.

I would add that while I have mostly talked about these bucket needs and tasks from the point of view of midlife people, these needs and tasks are valid for all relationships at any age. The same needs and tasks apply whether you are twenty, forty, sixty or eighty. As you can see, there is a lot of learning that needs to be done. From time to time I hear people criticize the current generation for expecting too much from its relationships. Some say it is absolutely unrealistic to expect that we can begin a relationship in our early to middle twenties and maintain a high-quality loving relationship for fifty or sixty years. I do not think that the expectation itself is unrealistic. I think that what is unrealistic is the notion that all of that will happen just because we would like it to be that way. Do we really want to settle for a situation in which people will have two, three, or four marriages or committed relationships in their lifetimes? Do we not see the damage that is done when family continuity is hopelessly destroyed and children have to adapt to so many step-relationships in their lives? I have had as one of my clients a ten-year-old girl who has to deal with twelve different grandparents! I am in favor of marital commitments that are for life, and I say that as someone who has gone through divorce and remarriage. As happy as I am now in a second marriage that has celebrated a twentieth anniversary, I would rather have had this happiness without the pain of divorce. There will always be divorce, of course. For countless reasons, we are bound to make mistakes, and there will be situations in which divorce will be the best of all the bad remedies. But I am not in favor of lowering our expectations. Keep the expectations high, but understand that happy, fulfilling relationships can be experienced only to the degree that we are willing to work at them. Nothing great happens by accident, and loving is no exception. We need to know how to do it, and we need to work constantly at it to meet the high expectations we have set. We can transform a ho-hum relationship into an exciting and fulfilling one. We can renew and regenerate a lifeless marriage into one that is satisfying and challenging. There is no better time to do this than at midlife. Just how to go about doing that is the subject of the next chapter.

Part Three
Midlife
Relationships

Chapter Six
Renewing Marriage at Midlife

We are learning that renewing or transforming your marriage relationship needs to begin around the time the first child goes off on their own and be completed shortly after the launching of the last one. This is because one of the strongest rationales for the continuity of marriage ends when the children leave home. By the time all of their children are out on their own, many parents have invested a great deal of energy, not to mention financial resources, in getting that task done. There are some marriages in which it seems that precious little else is holding the marriage together; but even where that is not the case, even where a marriage has something else going for it besides raising the children, it seems a good idea to work on revitalizing the marital bond by the time the children are launched.

A century ago, this revitalization was not as important as it is today. In the early 1900s the time between the marriage of the last child in a family and the death of the first parents was less than a year. Now a parental couple can look forward to more than sixteen years of married life after the marriage of all their children. In other words, we are living longer, and therefore our marriages need to be maintained for a longer period of time. This is also happening at a time when people are considering broadening their lives with new experiences rather than maintaining the same level of activity they had before the children were gone. Today at midlife, many persons are looking forward to investigating and moving into completely different areas of life, things they have postponed or delayed, and these changes mean that new demands will be made on a marriage relationship.

In addition, as Paulina McCullough and Sandra Rutenberg remind us in the chapter they contributed to *The Changing Family Life Cycle*, the population we call middle age will mushroom to seventy-five million persons by the year 2010, and that number will make up twenty-five percent of the nation's population. Even if the divorce rate remains constant, there will still be a higher incidence of divorce for midlife people. Nobody believes that the rate will remain the same or decline. They also point out that, in 1982, eleven percent of divorces or annulments were for individuals who had been married twenty years or more. Because of the large midlife population we will have by the end of the first decade of the new century, and because the divorce rate itself is likely to rise, marriage renewal is becoming a more serious issue.

It would be nice if some kind of periodic review of our marriage relationships were built into the structure of the institution of marriage. We have annual physicals, annual pap smears, annual blood test levels, and annual mammograms, all of which are a good idea. We have annual reviews at the places where we work that are, often intended to address any issues that have developed over the past year and to set some specific career objectives for the coming year. There seems to be no model for anything similar for our marriages, but there ought to be. Important issues arise in marriages also, and sometimes they are crucial. Sometimes objectives are accomplished in marriages, too, and we might benefit from discussing ways in which we could take the quality of our marriage up another notch in the coming year. The great majority of couples coming to me have had some premarriage counseling from the minister who performed their ceremony, but they have not had any professional assistance in looking at their marriage since then. In the first session, I ask each person to identify what he or she thinks are the major issues that have led to marital problems. Most can do so readily, and most of the time, both agree on the major issues. They may rank them differently, but few have any serious disagreements as to what the conflicted issues are. When I ask how long these issues have been present, the answer I get is always a long time. I would fall out of my chair if someone's response was, "since two weeks ago Thursday." It is usually at least eight to ten years, and more times than I can remember, it has been "since before the wedding."

More than half of the time, by my estimation, when a midlife couple comes to see me, one of the two has already decided that the most likely scenario for the future is the termination of the marriage. That person is coming to me as a last resort. He or she does not expect that anything will be learned in the process of counseling that will result in the transformation of the marriage. Sometimes, one person has decided to terminate the marriage, has already been to see the lawyer, and is coming on the lawyer's advice. That person may see me as a potential enemy. Marriage counselors are perceived as saving marriages, so if you don't want your marriage saved the marriage counselor may have an agenda contrary to yours. This is why in the first session I usually tell a couple that saving a marriage is not my agenda. My agenda is teaching a couple how to save their marriage if they want to.

When it is clear that, for one of the people, the marriage is indeed over, I suggest that each of them still has a major benefit to be experienced from cooperating fully in the counseling process. People recover from broken relationships quicker if they understand why they came apart. And I suggest that what we will be doing is more like an autopsy that is done on a patient after death to determine all of the factors that contributed to the cause of death.

Many people who come to counseling, however, as discouraged and unhappy as they may be, still have some flicker of hope that perhaps their marriage can be saved. Jim and Debbie made an appointment to see me the day after returning from taking their last child, Nicole, to visit the college that was her first choice. The daughter was just beginning her senior year in high school.

Jim and Debbie had been married for twenty-two years. Debbie says that she has been very unhappy for the last five or six years. Jim has given her no emotional support in their marriage at all. He has no interest in her or in their marriage, she believes. In the last ten years, he has had two extended and one brief affairs with other women. Yet Jim insists he does not want his marriage to end. He is coming to counseling because he would like me to help them "put this marriage back together." Debbie, on the other hand, does not believe it can be put back together and has endured the past five years so as not to disrupt the lives of their children. Now that Nicole is ready for college, she is ready to move out. To my question, "What would you like me to do for you?" her answer is, "give me some good reason why I should not go ahead with the divorce." She clearly does not think that I will manage to do that, but she will be able to tell her family that she got a "professional" opinion that her marriage was indeed dysfunctional and she is merely acting on professional advice. I do not detect much hope in Debbie that her marriage can be saved, but there is a good reason why she, and all those in similar situations, should invest herself fully in the counseling. Debbie is forty-two years old, an accomplished administrative assistant, and attractive. She will probably not want to be alone for the next forty years of her life. She is probably thinking that she will get out of this unhappy marriage, meet someone else, and experience the marriage she thought the first one was going to be. And indeed she may.

My concern however, for Debbie and for thousands like her, is that she is still the victim of that American mystique of love which tells her that the mistake she made was not finding the one who was right for her. This marriage has failed because they were not right for each other; a new one will work because this time she will find "Mr. Right." Let me be quick to add that there are just as many men as women who come to me believing that the best solution to an unhappy marriage is to dissolve it and create a new relationship with someone else. My belief is that most people who have been in an unhappy marriage for several years figure it is easier to start over with someone new than to try and fix something that has been broken for quite a while.

It is to those people that I need to say that such a rationale is not correct. It is not easier to build a happy relationship with someone new than it is to fix one that is broken. I believe it is just as hard. It will take as much time and energy, and you will have to work on many of the same issues that are present in your existing marriage. The only thing you will not have to do with someone new is to deal with the history of pain and wounding that you have in your present marriage. Dissolve your miserable marriage if you will, but do not think it will be so much easier with someone else. In fact, if you do not understand your own contribution to the misery of the existing marriage, you are very likely to end up in a second marriage with many of the same issues and once again be very unhappy.

That said, let me turn to the real focus of this chapter, which is how people may go about renewing their marriage at midlife. Here I am not talking only about a marriage that is in trouble, but about any and every marriage. However good and satisfying your marriage is as you approach midlife, it can be better. You can make it even more satisfying, more fulfilling. And why not? We only get one life in this world, so why settle for less than the most you can possibly get out of your primary source of love?

THE IMPORTANCE OF SELF-DIFFERENTIATION

The first step toward renewing your marriage at midlife is to take a serious look at where you are in terms of your self-differentiation. As I indicated in chapter one, midlife is one of those times when some pressure to "be a self" makes itself felt. It may be somewhat easier to raise your level of self-differentiation at midlife than at any other time, because people then are more mature and there is a heightened sense of life that is passing on.

Raising your level of self-differentiation actually begins with your relationship with your parents. Most of us have experienced that our parents have certain expectations of us. These can be very specific without our thinking that they want to run our lives. For example, they expect us to go to college, but to make our own choice of a career. They expect us to be married, but to choose our own spouse. They expect us to be active citizens, but don't expect to control our vote. Their influence may be stronger when it comes to a faith. They may expect us to continue in the faith tradition in which we were raised and be upset when we move to another faith tradition. Even when that occurs, I find that most parents come to terms with it over time.

There are some parents who are much more dominant, of course, and who do exert tremendous pressure on their children in regard to where they go to college, what they major in, what career they choose, whom they marry, where they live, what kind of house they buy, what career moves they should make, and so on. I worked with an extended family once in which the patriarch of the family, a grandfather, would sign his grandchildren up for tennis or golf lessons without even telling the parents. That kind of parental or grandparental influence is clearly wrong and inappropriate. Thank goodness that most of us do not have to deal with that kind of pathological attempt to control us.

Nevertheless, many people still have a lot of anxiety about their parents' approval and understanding long after they have moved into adulthood. I still see people in their forties and fifties who are concerned about what their parents will say about decisions they are making. I have seen divorces postponed until a parent is deceased for fear of disapproval. More often, I hear that the news of a divorce "will kill my father, mother, etc." I have seen plenty of pain that a divorce causes in a family, but I have never seen it kill anyone.

Self-differentiate from Your Parents

The first people from whom you need to differentiate yourself are thus your parents. If that job has already been done it does not ever need to be done again. If it has not been done, midlife is a good time to do it. Differentiation is done by clearly articulating to your parents what you think, what you believe, or what you are going to do, what you are not going to do, and then following through in spite of any efforts on their part to control what you think, believe, or do. It also means staying connected to them and refusing to be alienated from them in spite of themselves. This last level is a lot more difficult to achieve if we get a constant message of disapproval, but highly self-differentiated people do not cut themselves off from people with whom they disagree or from whom they receive some criticism, especially from one's parents.

I emphasize that the point of doing the work of differentiating yourself from your parents is not to persuade them to your point of view, your way of thinking, your feelings, or your way of doing anything. The goal is simply to be as clear as you can be in relation to them as to what you think, feel, and want to do. You are not seeking their approval, and you are not trying to alienate yourself from them. You have done a good job of self-differentiation if you are not emotionally reactive to either their approval or their criticism.

Self-differentiate from Your Spouse

The second task is to self-differentiate yourself in relation to your spouse. To some degree all of us modify some things about ourselves in order to please our spouses. There is nothing wrong with this as long as we do not give up essential aspects of our identity and as long as we do so consciously and intentionally. We may also not develop certain aspects of ourselves because we sense that this might affect the relationship with our spouses in a negative way. We always develop, grow, and expand in our relationship with others, and it is not always possible to keep our spouses informed with every little change that we make. For example, at some time I may have very clearly taken some position on the choice of living together without being married and shared that position with my wife. Over the years, I may slowly but surely see that issue as much more complicated than I once did, or I may reverse my thinking altogether and come to a more liberal position. I can think of a number of positions I have taken on theological issues in which my thinking has changed considerably from fifteen years ago, but in the day-to-day hustle and bustle I may not have let my wife in on a new nuance that I now perceive on some of those issues.

That is why midlife is a good time to make sure that, on the important issues that affect our relationship, my wife is clear as to what I think, believe, and want to do. Not every issue is that important to the relationship, but some are; and that is particularly true if it is a core issue as far as the relationship is concerned.

Midlife couple Phil and Dottie came for counseling because their marriage had become a lot more conflicted lately. Phil was an attorney; Dottie had been a full-time homemaker. There were four children in the family. Both Phil and Dottie were college graduates, and they had met in college. Both had come from very traditional family backgrounds. Dottie was an elementary school teacher, and she taught for the first three years of their marriage. With the first pregnancy, she had quit work and never returned. As the children got older and presented fewer demands, Dottie got involved in volunteer work in the community and found it very satisfying. Phil had been very happy with this arrangement for many years. They had agreed before the children came along that, in order to do the best they could for them, Dottie should be a full-time mother and homemaker. As a result, Dottie was completely taken by surprise and became irate when, in the course of an interview, Phil expressed his resentment that Dottie had never gone back into teaching. She felt, and rightly so, that she had been completely blindsided. Phil, rather sheepishly, admitted that he had only suggested this as an option, but he thought that she would hop at the suggestion since she had enjoyed teaching so much in the beginning. Phil insisted that he had never changed his position, but he certainly had not done a good job about being clear about what he thought and believed and how that was changing as the children got older. He admitted that he was afraid (i.e. too anxious) to bring it up directly, for fear that Dottie would think he was being controlling. Self-differentiated people do not let their anxiety about what the other will think or feel get in the way of clarifying what they think, believe, and will or will not do.

It could have been quite the opposite. Suppose, for instance, that Dottie had agreed that it would be good to be a full-time mother, but as soon as the youngest was in school she had a strong desire to pursue her career once again.

She might have been the one with the anxiety, afraid that Phil might think she was reneging on their agreement. She might have slowly built up resentment that she had given up her career while he was allowed to pursue his. They could have come to counseling at midlife with Dottie being the one who was upset, not him.

I show couples how to self-differentiate in relation to a spouse by drawing a large circle in the middle of a page and writing the word *issue* in the middle. Actually there are many issues, so you follow the same routine with each issue. You each define yourself in relation to that issue. And again, your task is not to persuade each other. You are not out to convince each other to your point of view; your task is simply to be clear about what you think, believe, want to do, or don't want to do. Obviously self-differentiation does not involve issuing ultimatums; there is no threat to end the connection if one does not do what the other one wants. That is control, not self-differentiation. The only expectation that you have in the process of self-differentiation is that your spouse will be consistent. You may discover that you share many of the same beliefs and that there is no conflict on the belief level. The conflict, if any, will show up at the "what I want to do" level. But now a compromise is possible because strategies, not beliefs, are involved: and strategies may be compromised more easily than beliefs. That way, whatever you decide to do, you will each be clear about what the other thinks, feels, believes, wants to do, or does not want to do. You will be surprised how much this will improve your communication, because it reduces the anxiety and the defensiveness that creates so much havoc in relationships.

Self-differentiate from Grown Children

The next step is for midlife couples to self-differentiate in relation to their grown children. While it may sound strange to some, professionals believe that the capacity to do this is related to the history of one's self-differentiation from one's own parents. The point is that issues between us and our parents will show up again in the relationships we have with our children. It follows logically that difficulty in being self-differentiated with parents will probably affect our self-differentiation from our children, or them from us. Bruce and Thelma brought their sixteen-year-old daughter, Terry, in for counseling. Thelma and Terry were involved in chronic conflict. Terry was still dependent upon her mother to get her up for school and cajole her into doing her homework. Terry lied chronically about where she was going and what she was doing. A neat triangle was created with the mother and daughter brought close by their conflict and the father at the distant corner. Triangles are created to deal with the anxiety that builds up between two persons. The creation of a triangle serves to siphon off some of the anxiety that one or both of the up-close persons are feeling. But triangles also serve to cause a relationship to become stuck, which was the case in this family.

The family-of-origin workup revealed that, at that very age, Thelma was locked in an almost identical pattern of conflict with her own mother. The situation had never been resolved, and so it was being acted out again in the next generation. I suggested several strategies. First, I tried a structural adjustment by arranging for the daughter to have to go to her father instead of mother with all her requests for permission, or money, but this did not work because the parties just could not stick to it. The only thing that was accomplished was that Dad became a lot more sympathetic to what his wife was dealing with. Next I tried coaching the mother to self-differentiate in relation to her daughter. In particular, I wanted her to spell out to her daughter what she would and would not do in terms of bailing her out of absences, late arrivals, missed assignments, and failed tests. As hard as she tried, Thelma could not follow through on what she said she would do or not do. What I now believe I should have done was go back to Terry and work on her self-differentiation with her mother. If that had happened, she might have been more capable of doing that with her daughter later.

In the course of raising our children, we begin from a situation of absolute dependence and ideally grow to the point where our children are independent of us in every way. Circumstances of life in middle-class America are such that our children are at least financially dependent upon us until their mid-twenties, some even longer. We are also experiencing what some call "boomerang children," that is, children who have left home, worked, and lived independently, or begun their own marriage and family, only to lose their job or go through a divorce and return home to regroup. The boomerang child who returns for six to twelve months while getting his or her life together is becoming more and more common. But the temptation is there for parents to do too much, and suddenly a mother whose children were launched has become the caretaker of her grandchild. For a brief period of time, this does not pose a big problem; but if it creates a long-standing dependency, it does not bode well for the marriage of grandma and grandpa.

An additional problem is that in some parental marriages, there is a tendency for women who experience the lack of emotional closeness with a spouse to fill that need through emotional closeness with her children. This may result in a serious delay in the launching of the last child, and that is even more likely if that last child is the third child in the family. (The third child in a family is often "wired" to the marriage relationship of the parents.) Sometimes the child may delay the launching, as if intuiting that he or she is all that is holding the marriage together; or the parent may unconsciously delay the launching so as not to be deprived of his or her source of emotional support.

What family professionals want to see happen is that the dependency nature of the parent/child relationship develops into an interdependent adult to adult relationship. The family tie is still strong and meaningful, but without one being emotionally or financially dependent upon the other. The best way to go about establishing an adult to adult relationship with our children is to do exactly what we have done with our own parents. We communicate clearly to them what we think, believe, feel, will do, and will not do, and we encourage them to do the same. My oldest son, Mark, called me around the 1997 Christmas holiday to let me know that his and his wife's Christmas plans did not include a stop at our home. My words to him were (I hope clearly), "Mark, it is not my expectation that you and Joy will spend every Christmas holiday with us. You have your own home now, and Joy has family, too. You may even want to not be with any family once in a while, so that the two of you can have some relaxing time together. You two were here for Thanksgiving, which we enjoyed very much, so do not feel that you have to be sorry for not being here for Christmas." I hope that my son and daughter-in-law got the message that I enjoy having them visit us, but that my enjoyment of any particular holiday is not dependent on their presence.

Our adult children will and do have problems, and we would be heartless parents if we did not expect to provide emotional and even financial support at times. But I also trust that all of us want our children to be financially and emotionally independent of us. We want them to be able to deal with the world, meet their own objectives, make successful relationships, and be able to take care of themselves without having to turn to us for advice or financial rescue.

Come To Terms with Career and Achievement

Midlife is also a time when both men and women, but especially men, need to come to terms with the arena of career and achievement. I say *especially men* because men in America are socialized to put the best of themselves into their work. From the time they are quite young, little boys are asked what they are going to *be* when they grow up. Please notice that. It is *be*, not *do*. *Be* is an ontological word; it is about essence and identity. From the time boys are quite young, they know that they are expected to work and to provide for someone other than themselves. Most little girls expect to get married, and they may wonder whether they will work outside the home or be full-time homemakers; and they know that, if they marry, they may work full- or part-time. Little boys never even imagine that they have as many alternatives. Married or single, they will work full time. Children or not they will work full-time. Whether a wife works full- or part-time, they will work full-time.

One of the questions I ask in the family-of-origin workup is to have my clients describe their fathers. The most frequent first response I hear is "hard worker." No other answer even comes close to that one. For better or worse men in America are raised to believe that they will find their ultimate meaning, significance, and destiny in their work. Sam Osherson, in a fine book called, *Finding Our Fathers: the Unfinished Business of Manhood*, suggests that since we saw our fathers work so much and so hard, we sons pour ourselves into our own work to see if we can find what it was that was so fulfilling or fascinating about work for them.

By midlife, I believe, men have either discovered what this was or found that it was an illusion. Some have discovered the exhilaration of accomplishment; for others, it is utter despair. I was surprised to read Studs Terkel's book *Working*, and discover that most of his respondents despised their work. I must say that I have always been blessed with the ability to find something that I have liked very much about the various careers and career settings I have worked in. If a man's work is filled with such lack of meaning and fulfillment, by midlife he cannot wait to retire. And even if it is exhilarating, a man finds that such exhilaration does not mean everything to him anymore. He still feels that there is something that is missing, that life is more than work, no matter how satisfying.

The midlife man today has one tremendous advantage over his counterpart a century earlier. He has a much better chance of getting out of an unhappy and unfulfilling career and getting into one that provides more satisfaction. Some men go back to school at night or on weekends and gear up for a new career. Dreams that have been neglected can, at midlife, still be acted on. We are not stuck as our fathers and grandfathers were.

My point is that midlife is a time for a man to do an honest assessment of his investment in his career. In many cases, by midlife a man has gotten as far as he is going to go, or as far as he wants to go. Now may be the time to follow that passion for something that the demands of supporting a family have never allowed him to do. Now is also the time to take some of that career investment and redirect it to his marriage relationship.

Meanwhile, women at midlife often have an opposite, but equally important problem. They have invested the best of themselves in their marriages and in their children. They have done this, in some cases, even while working outside the home full- or part-time. This is also a time for them to do some assessment. Have they been nursing a passion to return to the full-time career they left when the children came along? Is this the time to go back to school and finish the major that was left unfinished, or to pursue the major that was exchanged for something more "practical" at the time? Or is there just a desire for knowledge for the sake of knowledge? The early socializing patterns of women in our culture used to prepare them to look for their meaning in life in their relationships, rather than in their achievements in the business world. This is undoubtedly why many women suppressed their need for achievement in the first half of life. The feminist movement has done much to change that socializing pattern, with the result that many women are succeeding in careers once populated mostly by men.

Both partners thus have some self-differentiating to do, and they need to keep the lines of communication wide open between them as they go about it. This is the first step in renewing and renegotiating the marriage relationship—to do some unfinished work with their parents, with each other, with their children, with their career choices, and with desires for the future.

THE RELATIONSHIP'S HISTORY

The second step in marital renewal is to do a careful review of the history of the relationship from the beginning of the courtship. What do you remember about how you met, about what you did on the first date, and about how soon you decided to make your relationship an exclusive relationship? What kind of conflicts, if any, did you have in the early stages of your relationship? How were those conflicts resolved? How did your parents like your choice of girl-friend, or boyfriend? Most important of all, perhaps, is recalling what it was about the other that attracted you and influenced you not only to continue the relationship, but to move toward a life-long relationship.

One of the most important purposes behind these kinds of questions is to help people remember some of the excitement and exuberance that was there early in their relationship. As unhappy as a relationship may be at the moment, there was a time when it was much happier. Recalling some of the features and characteristic behaviors that were there in the beginning, may give some very good clues about what needs to be put back into a relationship. One woman happily recalled how her lover used to pick her up every morning for work, how he never failed to call her at least once in the morning and once in the afternoon. "About eight months after the wedding, it suddenly occurred to me that you were not doing that any more. It made me sad." Others can remember how they used to talk for hours and how they could not believe how fast the time seemed to pass.

The initial attraction is important too. Physical attributes often play a large part in the very early attraction—he was handsome; she was beautiful—but I do not think that physical attractions alone are enough to keep people together beyond the first few dates. Other kinds of experiences have to come along. "He really seemed to know where he was going in life." "She was so easy to talk to." "She was very intelligent and not afraid to be that way." "I was impressed with the way his family was so close." "He introduced me to the larger world out there." Those are some of the responses I have heard.

Did you have any serious conflicts before the wedding? What were the issues? How did you resolve them? Or did you just agree on a cease-fire instead of resolving the conflicts? After forty years of taking marital histories, I can say that, without exception, most of the serious conflicts that show up in a marriage later were experienced in some form already in the courtship. And the pattern of resolving conflicts, or the lack of a strategy for conflict resolution, began there too.

It is also helpful at midlife to recall the variety of characteristics that attracted us to each other, because it can make very clear some of the things that have changed—or some of the things that are still the way they were in the beginning. Julia told me she was originally attracted to Charlie because he introduced her to the excitement of auto racing. Five years later, Charlie was still into the excitement of auto racing; in fact he was all over the country doing just that while she felt cooped up with two children under the age of four. His exciting car racing had another side to it; or what had been a positive had changed, for her, into a negative. So recalling the early courtship period of the relationship gives us the opportunity to reflect on what has changed and what is still the same.

There are some other important times in one's marital history that it helps to reflect on. The first year of married life is important. Where did you live? Where did you work? Do you remember the first year as a happy one? How did you adapt from living at home, or alone, to living together? Were there any serious conflicts in the first year of marriage? Were these conflicts that you had already dealt with in courtship or new ones? How did you resolve them? Most couples think that their problems have surfaced only in the last five or so years, but answers to these questions can help them see that some of their current problems are not new, but may have been around for a long time. And both people can see how they have each played a part in ignoring or failing to come up with effective strategies in the past.

A very important question about the first year of marriage is whether or not married life was pretty much what you expected it to be or not. If not, what was different? I find that expectations of what married life is going to be like change with life experiences. High school romances that move right into marriage upon graduation have expectations that are often naïve, as though married life is pretty much like a date that does not end. It is in the first years of marriage that we make the biggest adjustment of all, namely from "I thinking" to "We thinking." Forty percent of all divorces occur within the first five years of marriage. I contend that those figures indicate that people's expectations of each other, or of the marriage relationship, were anything but realistic.

I do not expect couples to be able to go through this recall process on a year-by-year basis. Unless you kept a diary, you usually can't separate one year from another; but there are some important events that make certain years and times more important than others. The year of the first pregnancy is important. How did the marital adjustment shift around the birth of your first child?

And again, what was good and what was not so good about your marriage at that time? Years in which major moves occurred, or major job changes, six months of unemployment, the year in which a life-threatening sickness or accident occurred, the year in which the first loss of one of your parents had to be grieved. How did you handle that crisis? How did your marriage change? Was there something good that was missing after that? Were there some new anxieties or resentments?

In this whole assessment of the marital history, it is important to go back to the five buckets of need I have identified, as well as to the five tasks that are necessary in a loving relationship. One partner can often see quite plainly that it was after some particular experience that the other's attention bucket began to be neglected, or someone became very conscious of the loss of the feeling of equality. And again, the point is that what was missing and when it began to be missing suggest quite simply what needs to be added back into the relationship. If it was never there, it needs to be.

After the past has been explored, it is time to turn toward our expectations for the future. If it is appropriate, past mistakes can be acknowledged, confessed, or forgiven, but not forgotten. Trying to forget the past won't work, it needs to be forgiven; and forgiveness is easier than forgetting any day. But now it is time to move on. What kinds of expectations does each person have about how their future relationship will be lived out.

Once more, I suggest going back to those buckets. "I need more attention." "I need to have my separateness honored better than it has been in the past." I press people for clarity and objectivity. I saw Clarice for several sessions after she separated from her husband. She came for counseling because she needed to sort out her feelings and make a decision about whether she was going to return to the marriage or not. She said she was going to "see how my husband handles the separation." Her husband was unemployed and attempting to collect disability benefits for an injury. He could not return to his former employment because it required a lot of physical exertion, but she believed that he was capable of employment, that he was a very intelligent person, and that she could not tolerate his not working at all. She was also angry at the way he related to one of their children. After several sessions, I suggested that since the end of the time line she had given herself was approaching, it might be more helpful to her husband if she gave him a very clear and specific idea of what her expectations were, instead of just waiting to see how he would handle the separation. Since he wanted her to come back, why not give him a list of the expectations that she would have to see met before she would come back and invite him to give her a similar list of what his expectations were if she did come back. She gave him her list, which had at the top that she expected him to get a job, at least part-time. There were several other items on the list as well. Two days after he got the list, he filed for a divorce. That may not have been a happy outcome, but my point is that once the situation became clear, something was resolved.

A midlife couple owes it to each other to set the agenda, the priorities for the second half of their lives and for their marriage. One of the main tasks that has kept them together, namely raising the children is complete, and the question now is what we want to do with the rest of the marriage. This takes time; it takes some reflection; and it takes all the other things mentioned in this chapter. I believe that reading some books about marriage might be in order, and some suggested readings are included at the back of this book. It might be a wise idea to look for a counselor who could facilitate this process. Community colleges and other educational institutions in your area may offer a course you could audit. Attend a Marriage Encounter weekend, or a marriage enrichment program. Both are available almost anywhere in our country. Churches often offer courses in their adult education department.

Not all couples, of course, have children. Some, for medical reasons cannot have children; others choose not to. These people still face the same midlife challenges as do people with children. They will need to use the same process that I have spelled out in this chapter to renew their relationships.

When it is all done, and assuming you are going to have a second marriage with the same spouse with whom you had in your first one, I suggest you think about a Renewal of Marriage Ritual. Symbols and rituals are powerful. They mark transitions, beginnings, and endings, and they give a spiritual and metaphysical boost to our minds, hearts, and souls. In the ancient world, there were many more rituals than today, and we are the poorer for our lack. Most churches have rituals already printed for the renewal of marriage vows, or new ones can be written. The ritual may be limited to the family, or include neighbors, close friends, and even business associates. The old wedding pictures can be dusted off and put on display. Pictures of the children as babies, going off to school, graduating from high school and college, getting married and having their own children could be included. Awards, trophies, and accomplishments can be displayed. As a priest, I would like to see the whole celebration be surrounded by a worshipping community, but it can also be done in the home. Wedding anniversaries often get celebrated by the family, but somehow the recommitment of a couple to a renewed and transformed marriage is something more important to celebrate than a marriage that has simply been endured for a certain number of years.

Chapter Seven
Divorce and Recovery at Midlife

Divorces are always stressful. On the Holmes/Rahe Stress Scale, near the top of life events that produce stress. In forty years of counseling with people before, during, and after a divorce, I have yet to see what some people call an "easy divorce." At any time in our lives, the divorce process is an emotionally draining experience. It is fraught with intense anxiety, and sometimes the anxiety lasts for weeks, if not months. Even when the divorce is a relief to at least one of the spouses, the anxiety is still there. Divorce is a major disruption in one's personal life, and of course the disruption affects not only the individuals, but entire extended families. Given that there are 3,200 divorces in America each day, and that those divorces involves an average of one child each, it means one day's divorces affect 9,600 persons at a minimum. In most cases, there are parents, brothers and sisters who are also affected. Patterns of friendship and work systems are affected as well.

There are a number of realities of divorce that make it stressful no matter how long the marital history is. One of the realities most neglected in the books that are written about divorce is that the actual circumstances of the divorce—that is, whether or not you are the one seeking the divorce—can make all the difference in the world. The initiator of the divorce is in an emotional context radically different from the one who is being divorced. In the great majority of divorces, one person wants the divorce and one person wants the marriage to continue. These opposite circumstances result in two very different emotional realities.

The party who initiates the divorce deals primarily with guilt feelings. No matter how much we may say or think otherwise, divorce feels like a failure, and initiators cannot escape the feeling that they are the perpetrators of that failure and its consequences. In addition, the party who does not want the divorce always seems to know how to push the buttons that will activate those feelings of guilt powerfully. Initiators get asked questions like, "Why are you doing this to me?" "How can you do this to your children, your parents?" Frequently there has been a pattern of this spouse manipulating the other through guilt in the marriage relationship. If the spouse who has been manipulated is now the one initiating the divorce, he or she will often protect himself or herself by developing a cold, tough exterior. He or she will then be accused of being cold and unfeeling, totally lacking in compassion. Initiators will struggle with this for a long time, even after the divorce is final.

The one not initiating the divorce, on the other hand, deals primarily with the feeling of being abandoned or somehow flawed. "There must be something wrong with me," is the strongest perception these persons deal with. This usually leads to a bitter defensiveness. "I have been a good provider for my family," he insists. "I put my heart and soul into this home, and now she and the children are going to get to enjoy it and I will have to find some place else to live." That life is not fair is a maxim frequently heard during the divorce process. "I gave him the best years of my life," she says. "I stayed home with the children so that he could work as much as he wants to. Now the kids are gone. I don't have a career, and he is dumping me like so much garbage."

If the initiator already has a relationship with someone else, these feelings of guilt and abandonment are intensified. The initiator feels even more guilty for having broken a promise of fidelity, and the responder feels even more abandoned because the "replacement" is there for all to see. Both the feeling of guilt and the feeling of abandonment will be major obstacles to recovering from divorce; this is true at any time, but exacerbated at midlife.

THE REALITIES OF MIDLIFE DIVORCE
A Longer Marriage

There are several reasons why the problems and issues of divorce are even more severe at midlife. The first is that divorce at midlife means that the marriage relationship has a long history; most midlife divorces have a history of twenty to thirty years. Think of all of the experiences that are a part of the memories of that long a history. Think of all the shared experiences that have accumulated. Most marriages have had some good years before they began to go downhill. Family albums crammed full of pictures will never again give the pleasure they once did; they are now only reminders of what used to be that is now gone. All kinds of memorabilia scattered around the house, gleaned from vacation trips and other events, or from the lives of the children, all become reminders of what used to be. Symbols of family solidarity are transformed into symbols of brokenness and pain. Birthday gifts, anniversary presents, and furniture acquired together all become silent reminders of the tragedy. Marriages that have only a five-year history have not accumulated all those memories, but ones that have endured for twenty years or more have a lot of them. There is more to grieve, more memories and experiences that must be let go of.

Family Continuity

The second reality that makes divorce at midlife a more serious issue is the loss of continuity in the family. After twenty years or more, connections with extended family are often quite meaningful. Two brothers-in-law, or sisters-in-law may have become close friends. I have heard many husbands and wives tell me what a loss it is to them that they will not have the same relationship any more with a mother- or father-in-law. Some have become closer to their in-laws than to their own parents. Family reunions, though they seem to be dwindling these days, will never be the same after divorce. Aunt Lucille won't be bringing the potato salad that everyone has raved about for years. Fishing trips with cousins will gradually fade out. These are significant losses, and their loss will have to be grieved, too.

In addition, think of all the family traditions that are a part of the continuity of the family. In families where the adult children come "home" for Christmas or Thanksgiving, they now have to make arrangements to spend some time at Mom's and some time at Dad's. Often it is the same for birthday celebrations. Family weddings are now a problem, too. I attended a wedding once where the animosity was still so bad that instead of the traditional bride's and groom's sides, all of the fathers of the bride and groom were on one side and all the mothers were on the other side. Former wives refused to sit with former husbands, and so forth.

Economic Realities

The economic realities of midlife divorce are powerful and often tragic. Home equities must be divided, and investments must be liquidated, and often at a time when it may not be wise economically. Pensions, IRAs and 401Ks will be affected. In their book *Surviving the Breakup*, Wallerstein and Kelly have documented the consequences for midlife women, many of whom have not been in the workforce full-time. Former skills have become rusty, or worse yet have become obsolete because of rapid technological advances in the computer and office-machine fields. Many women face economic losses that they will never recover from. Men, of course, face economic losses too, but they seem to recover faster and better than women.

What we are talking about here are major changes in lifestyle. Often neither spouse can afford to stay in the family home, so it is sold, the equity divided, and both move into a smaller home or an apartment. Country-club membership is no longer available to one, sometimes to both. Favorite shopping places are no longer affordable. Dining out as often is impossible. Economic survival is often intense in a way not experienced since the first years of the marriage, only this time each is managing it alone.

The financial assistance available to help the children is also affected. Some are still in college or graduate school; some are just getting started in marriages and families of their own. The ability of midlife divorced persons to provide financial assistance to these children may either end completely or be seriously curtailed, and that, in turn, can create some serious resentment leveled at one or both of the parents.

Adult children may have resentment of quite a different kind. In one case, a thirty-year-old son informed his mother that he would not have any further relationship with her because she chose to leave his father for another man. In many cases, I deal with adult children who do not want to meet the other woman that Dad is involved with, or will see their father only if she is not around. Mom and Dad may be invited to their grandchildren's birthday parties, but are told not to bring the new boyfriend or girlfriend. Forbidding the "other" man or woman at family celebrations often continues to be the rule even after Dad or Mom is remarried, creating considerable stress on the re-marriage, as well.

Social Patterns

An especially troublesome reality of divorce at midlife are the changes in social and friendship patterns. After twenty years of marriage, most of a couple's friends are other married couples, and most of their social outlets involve doing things with couples. After divorce, however, you are no longer part of a couple, so you are often not invited to the social functions of your friends because their gatherings are for couples. Besides, what I have noticed is that, over time, former friends of a couple gravitate toward one, but not both persons who were formerly a couple. It is just too difficult to remain close friends of both.

If the social network of a couple consisted of people associated with the husband's work and career, most of them will probably gravitate toward him. The consequence is that a divorced midlife woman may suddenly find herself without a support network, because her former friends have continued to stay in close contact with her ex-husband and have chosen to let their friendship with her fizzle out. Having left her husband, or having been abandoned by her husband, she must build a new social network. Most women can do this, but it takes time; and in the critical first year of separation and divorce, she is left without much support.

On the other hand, for many couples, the task of keeping an active social life has been done by the woman. When that is the case, and when the social network is more varied, it is more likely that the husband may be the one finding himself without much of his former social life with other couples. Men, however, tend to compartmentalize their friendships. They have at-work friends, neighborhood friends, golf friends, and church friends. Male friendships are more superficial and seldom involve deep and lasting connections. Men are indeed the poorer emotionally because of their lack of intimate friendships and thus may experience a crushing loneliness as a consequence of their decision to leave the marriage, or of having been left by a wife.

For both men and women, the reality is that while some of their former friendships will survive and some will not, most of the former friends will not remain friends with both. As a result, if your social network is devastated, you must begin to build a new one, but doing so is not easy when you have not had to work at it consciously for a long time.

This is why both men and women going through divorce gravitate toward support groups made up of people going through the same experiences. There are national groups such as Parents Without Partners and Solo Parents. The latter tends to be made up of younger people who still have young children at home. Many midlife people do attend the large regional meetings of Parents Without Partners, but in many local chapters, the focus may be on support for younger single parents. My experience is that the quality of the programming, and the group experience itself, varies widely from region to region. I have seen some local chapters that have great leadership, plan and execute outstanding programs, and have built up strong programs that give excellent emotional and educational support to people going through divorce. There are, sad to say, some local programs with poor leadership and poor programming.

In many communities there are individual counselors who function as facilitators for small divorce support groups. Many of these are excellent, and they do not cost as much as individual counseling sessions would. There are usually churches in larger communities that also offer some high-quality divorce recovery groups. They arrange to bring in experts, such as people in banking and finance to give financial advice, or childhood experts to provide advice on dealing with children as a custodial or noncustodial parent. Again, these programs are usually not too costly. If money is not a problem, there are counselors who specialize in individual divorce recovery counseling. There are, of course, tons of books on the subject available in bookstores and libraries. Many of these are very good. Of the ones I have read, I believe that *Uncoupling* by Diane Vaughan, is the one that impressed me the most. Vaughan has managed to give a very realistic, step-by-step analysis of the process by which a marriage comes apart. I also recommend Wallerstein and Kelly's *Surviving The Breakup*.

GETTING THROUGH DIVORCE: THE GRIEF MODEL

Within the field of divorce therapy, there are two models used to help people understand and cope with the experience. The first of these, borrowed from the model made popular by Elizabeth Kübler-Ross in *Death And Dying*, is the grief model. I believe this is an appropriate model to use since there is something that is dead, something that is never going to exist again, and its absence needs to be grieved. A relationship is, for all practical purposes, dead. While there will still be some ongoing contact between former spouses, their relationship will be radically different from what it had been in the past. It will be very sporadic. Ex-spouses will deal with each other around certain nodal events, such as weddings, graduations, funerals, births, and baptisms. For people at midlife, when children are already grown and on their own, there will not be much to require an ongoing relationship, so it needs to be grieved.

The shortcoming to this model is that it is a better paradigm for the one who does not want the divorce than for the one who does. The one who wants the divorce is not in a grieving mode at all; that may come later, but it will be much later. While going through the divorce process itself, the initiator is experiencing growing degrees of relief, not grief. I tend to use this model the most when, after some initial analysis of the marital history, my continuing client is the one who has not wanted the divorce and needs to recover from the grief of all the losses that will be involved for him or her.

Stage 1: Denial

There are five stages in the grief model. The first stage is characterized by denial. People say things like, "I can't believe this is happening." "Our marriage is not that bad." Sometimes responders are in denial because initiators are not completely honest. Many couples come to a counselor because one party wants a divorce, but does not tell the other. It is as though the initiator wants to transfer the responsibility for the emotional care of a spouse from himself or herself to the counselor. Jack made an appointment with me for himself and Tracy. The trigger for the decision was that Tracy found out that Jack was involved with a woman from work. When they came for counseling, Tracy knew that their marriage was in some serious trouble, but Jack was withholding from her that he had already decided to leave the marriage. He "knew" that Tracy would not handle it well, so he wanted to get a counselor involved. In the first session, I want to find out what the level of commitment to the continuation of the marriage is, and so I ask, "On a scale of one to ten, how hopeful are you that this marriage can be saved?" I could tell how uncomfortable Jack was with the question. Tracy could tell too, and it was easy to see that her anxiety was approaching a panic level. Tracy wanted to deny what was very obvious. The next day, Jack called to let me know that his strategy was to let Tracy down gradually, that his plan was to slowly reveal more and more of his desire to leave the marriage. I told him I thought that was like doing an amputation with a dull knife; and besides, it would encourage Tracy to hang on to the denial longer. Jack was actually a lot more worried about dealing with his own discomfort about Tracy's anger than anything else, so I suggested he, too, would be better off facing the anger and getting on with it.

Stage 2: Anger

This example reveals the second stage of the grief model, anger. In the anger stage, there is a lot of accusation and name calling. Threats are often made also. The anger is necessary because we have been hurt, deeply hurt. Anger may actually function as the scissors that cuts through some of the emotional cords that are tying us to someone else; and if there is going to be a divorce, cutting through those emotional ties will be necessary. Thus venting anger is fairly healthy, I believe. I have worked with some clients who, up to ten years after their divorce, have never gotten into to anger stage, which clearly delays recovery. It is better to get angry, and begin to cut some of the emotional ties. The other possibility is that people get stuck here and ten years later have still not gone beyond the anger stage. You cannot move on with your life if you stay stuck in any of these early stages. Counseling may be needed to prevent getting stuck.

Stage 3: Bargaining

The next stage is the bargaining stage. This is where one spouse tries to make a deal with the other. If the initiating spouse will just stay, then the other promises to start doing this or to stop doing that. The presupposition of this stage is that, no matter what, I will be better off if the marriage stays together. The bargainer may be in a marriage that has been severely dysfunctional for a long time, but is so afraid of being alone that he or she is willing to promise anything just to keep the marriage together. "I will quit drinking." "I will get a different job." "I will give you more sex." "I will stop nagging." When this does not work, the bargainer may return to the denial or the anger stage. In fact, no one goes sailing through these stages one after another, you move back and forth a lot.

Stage 4: Acceptance

The next stage is the acceptance stage. At this stage the one who has not wanted the divorce and who has fought to keep it, finally recognizes that, however unwanted, divorce is going to happen. Even at this stage, one may return briefly to anger, denial, or bargaining, but over time he or she is becoming more and more resigned to the reality of a broken marriage. It is in this stage that the responder finally begins to make plans for the future that will not involve being married to the initiator. One by one, the consequences are dealt with and all of the realities begin to be considered. This results in the lowering of an anxiety that has been pretty high up to this point. Thoughtful, rational decisions are now possible, but it is not the final stage.

Stage 5: Letting Go

The final stage is called letting go. What is actually "let go" is all of the primary emotional connections. Letting go would mean the end of denial and anger altogether. Bitterness and resentment are gone. This stage has been reached when a person is finally able to put all of his or her energy into getting on with life instead of wistfully looking back. What lies ahead now, however unclear, looks better than what lies behind. There is the feeling that one is going to be OK, in some cases maybe better off than could have been imagined a few months earlier. One of the clues that tells me a person has gotten to this stage, besides the loss of bitterness and anger, is when I hear that, if the other person changed his or her mind, he or she would not be taken back.

How long does the divorce recovery process take? No one can say. It takes as long as it takes. I believe a reasonable amount of time to expect is twelve to eighteen months. Of course it is longer if you are not the initiator and the breakup comes as a surprise. I do not mean to say that after eighteen months one is no longer dealing with any of the emotional or financial consequences of a divorce; there may be financial realities that last for many years. For women, and sometimes for men, a divorce often means starting all over from scratch financially.

GETTING THROUGH DIVORCE: THE CRISIS MODEL

The other model that we use to help people understand the divorce process is the crisis model. The advantage of using this model is that it applies equally to both the initiator and the responder since it recognizes that both people are not necessarily grieving. This model is generally described as having four stages, but I prefer to add a fifth one.

Stage 1: Predivorce

The first stage is the *predivorce* stage. Diane Vaughan, in her book *Uncoupling* says that every divorce begins with a secret, and it is this secret that characterizes the predivorce stage. One of the parties is unhappy enough to consider terminating the marriage, but does not tell the other. That party may, in fact, already be involved with someone else. This is a period in which the storm clouds are gathering. One person is working on a plan to which the other is not privy. This may, in fact, be an unusually quiet and calm time, without some conflicts that have been a part of the daily routine of the relationship; but it is a false calm. Because they don't want to upset family celebrations for their children people wait till after a son or daughter is married, after a graduation, until Mom or Dad is gone, after the holidays, till the end of the school year.

Stage 2: The Acute Stage

The second stage of the crisis model is the acute stage. The secret is out. The desire of one spouse for the divorce is out in the open; the existence of an affair becomes known. In this acute stage, as one can imagine, things can get pretty crazy. There is loud conflict, and uncharacteristic behavior. Threats and accusations fly back and forth. Somebody moves out. Frantic calls are made to parents and/or friends. Things are just as chaotic for the initiator as for the responder, and the behavior of either one may be out of control for a period of time. Appetite and sleep are affected. This can be a very frightening time for the children.

Stage 3: The Sub-acute State

At some point the couple may make an appointment with a counselor or an attorney. This, I believe, ushers in a third stage that I call the sub-acute stage. None of the issues may be settled, and none of the anger or pain may yet be dealt with; but now there is a third party involved, or a fourth if each engages an attorney. The inclusion of a counselor or attorney siphons off some of the anxiety that is creating all of the erratic behavior. Both spouses are aware that "somebody else is watching." The conversations with lawyers or counselors help to reduce some of the anger, and a lot more rational thinking begins to take place. The length of this stage may depend on the laws of the state in which the couple resides. In my state (Iowa), a period of ninety days must pass between the filing of the petition to dissolve and the adjudication of that petition. At this point, if young children are involved, the state requires counseling in order to minimize the impact of the family's breaking up on the children. The ninety-day waiting period can be waived, but most people do not do it. Now the angry, anxious moments are interspersed with quieter times. Support networks are formed.

Stage 4: Transition

The next stage is the transition stage. In this stage, both of the spouses begin to make the adjustment to life without each other. Both parties may begin this stage before the divorce decree is issued, but usually it must wait until the final settlements have been made.

Stage 5: Stabilization

The final stage is the stabilization stage. At this stage, new routines are established. Old friendships are still there but new friendships may also be formed. Anxiety, anger, bitterness, and resentment have quieted down, if not disappeared. Life feels stable and predictable; the future is anticipated. Usually people are dating again, or feel confident and content without dating.

RECOVERING FROM DIVORCE

In spite of my suggestion that it takes twelve to eighteen months to get through the emotional upheaval of a divorce, I want to say that I am talking about reasonable expectations, not a time frame that everybody must follow. It takes as long as it takes. Nobody can get through all of this in six weeks, and while you ought to be through it in less than five years, no one can fix your time of recovery for you.

I do believe, however, that there are steps you can take to get through the process well, which is what the priority ought to be. It is not how quickly, but how well. Even if the midlife marriage is miserable, divorce is traumatic; and if you find yourself at fifty-two facing something you never thought you would have to face, you have a lot of life left to live, twenty to thirty years perhaps. But even if it turns out to be ten, you don't want to spend those ten years lonely and bitter.

Everyone going through a divorce should seek assistance from a counselor. Divorce counseling has become a sub-specialty under the general heading of marriage and family counseling. Counseling can keep you focused and prevent your wallowing in your grief for too long. Henrietta made an appointment with me because she said she was having a difficult time adjusting to her divorce. She just could not get on with her life. After telling her that getting over a divorce is not easy and that it takes time, I asked her how long ago she had been divorced. She said, "Ten years." "Why do you think that it is taking you so long to recover?" I asked her. She said, "You know, I think it's because I never found out why he divorced me." This was a good insight. People need to know why they were divorced. Henrietta and her husband had never seen a counselor, either in their married life or during the divorce process.

I suggested that she write her ex-husband a letter asking him. Why not hear it from the horse's mouth, so to speak? His answering letter became the starting point for our counseling sessions, during which we went through the history of the marriage. As I recall, we did this in three sessions. It might have taken longer without the letter from her divorced husband, but Henrietta knew now why she was divorced. She might not have agreed with it, but she knew. She called about a month after the last session to tell me she was grateful for the assistance, that she was doing well, and that she was going on the third date with a man whom she had been turning down for about a year. We do not recover from divorce if we don't know why. Counseling helps.

Attending support groups, going back to school, building a new network of friends, getting at least a part-time job—any and all of these may help. There are also these days some very high-quality singles organizations available that have excellent and helpful programs. Except for some rural areas, at least one of these organizations can be found in your community. Some meet under the auspices of churches, some under a community college sponsorship; some are sponsored by human service agencies in the community. Some are even formed specifically for professional people. Don't assume that the people who go to these groups are all in their thirties and forties. There is a good representation of people of all ages. In the beginning especially, I recommend looking into one of these groups.

All of the strategies about loving and renewal that I talked about in chapters five and six should be put to work, too. The same exercises that couples may go through to renew their marriage, midlife divorced people may use profitably to help them decide who they want to be for the rest of their lives. I suggest you return to those chapters and go through that material again, but this time with the focus just on your own life.

ADULT CHILDREN AND DIVORCE

There is a notion today that adult children are not affected by their parents' divorce the way young children are. It is true, of course, that our adult children do not experience the same kind of panic that young children do since they are on their own. Young children feel like the whole world is coming apart. They cannot sleep, sometimes lose their appetite, cannot concentrate in school, get into fights, become acutely depressed, and so on. We usually do not see these acute symptoms in adult children, but they are affected. They sometimes have problems with loyalty; indeed, parents sometime create those problems by demanding that the children share their hurt or turn against one of the parents. Even when that does not happen, adult children are affected. Some of them are married, and their parents' marital separation may bring to the surface problems that are simmering in their own marriages. Adult children should not be neglected, they need explanations, too.

Some parents have done a good job of hiding the dysfunctional nature of their marriage from their own children. Mike and Margaret had kept secret from their children the fact that when both of them were quite young, Mike had gotten into serious trouble because of a gambling addiction. He had gotten very deeply in debt and faced life-threatening consequences. Margaret had thought about leaving him then, but she felt guilty, she said, about "kicking a man when he's down." It was very tough financially; Mike even had to get some additional education. But with lots of help from both of their parents and a lot of scrimping, they got through it. From that time on, the marriage was really in a lot of trouble. Margaret felt very unappreciated by Mike. She had stood by him and stayed with him, but she was just as neglected emotionally after the upheaval as before. I saw Mike and Margaret at the point at which Mike had met another woman and decided to leave Margaret. The children, one in college and one in senior high school, could not understand what had happened until their parents sat down and told them the whole story. They still didn't like it, but they understood it.

STARTING OVER

Admittedly it is a lot easier to start over at twenty-five than at fifty-five, but it is still possible. Human beings are hard-wired to be resilient, and can be unless they have allowed themselves to be programmed otherwise.

If you are between forty and sixty and starting over there are some things you need to know. The first is not to be in a big hurry. In his book *Generation to Generation*, Edwin Friedman reminds us that the quicker we move to replace a loss, the less opportunity there is for growth. The story of Mike and

Margaret did not end, of course, when they revealed the depth of the problems in their marriage to their children. Two weeks after moving out of the
family home, Mike moved in with the woman he was having an affair with,
going from a marital home that has been dysfunctional for many years, right into
another relationship. That is too soon, and Mike will pay the price down the line.

After a divorce, it takes time to rebuild one's sense of self, one's identity.
There is a lot to be thought about. This is not a time for panic or for making
big decisions about your life. Mike may have wanted out of the relationship
very badly and assumes that he has nothing to grieve, but the giddiness of the
new relationship will keep Mike from working on discovering what all he has
done that contributed to the dysfunction of his marriage relationship. He has
some faulty relationship strategies that are going to affect this new relationship as badly as they affected his old one.

When is one ready to begin dating again? The answer is when most of the
emotional cords of the past have been cut. Many people need to realize that
anger and resentment can connect them to someone just as much as love. All
the emotional connections need to be cut, not just the positive ones. When
you lose someone emotionally close, you lose your sense of wholeness. You
will know you are doing a good job of recovering when a new sense of wholeness has begun to emerge. How can you tell? You can tell because the bitterness is gone, the anger is gone. The "letting go" is already in the past, but that
is all pretty subjective. Let me give you something a little more objective.

Every divorce requires the creation of what I call "the story." The story is
what I tell when someone asks, "What happened to your first marriage?" Or,
"Why did you get a divorce?" I have learned that the story changes through
the recovery process, and that by marking those changes you can tell where in
the recovery process you are. The first change is in the length of the story. In
the acute stage, the story is very long. It takes a long time to tell, and is full of
details of the time and what was said in conversations and all of that. Over
time, the story should get shorter. The painful details, the time of the day, the
day of the week, what he said or she said—all that stuff gets phased out of the

story. The story that used to take a good forty-five minutes to tell now can be told in five. I've seen it reduced to two or three words. "Why did you guys get divorced?" "He drank."

The other change that marks the degree of recovery is that the assignment of blame for the marriage not making it gets closer to fifty-fifty. In forty years of counseling, I have yet to see a marriage in which both people were not at fault on a nearly equal basis, certainly one too close to call. Besides, even if we could assign exact shares of blame, it would not mean anything. This is especially true in the case of a marriage that comes apart at midlife; both persons have contributed significantly to the dysfunction that was there. This does not mean that it's her fault if he has an affair; he had lots of choices he could have made. But he and she both contributed to the unhappy condition that was created, a condition in which both were probably making choices that only made the situation worse. Thus when the story is short and when you can acknowledge your contribution to the condition of the marriage, you can be pretty sure that you are ready to start over.

Being single again at midlife is a little scary at first, so I teach people about the art of reframing. Reframing is a way of looking at what you think is a negative reality and giving it a positive spin. Every ending implies that a new beginning is out there. A closed history can mean the beginning of a new adventure. A failed marriage implies the chance to build a new relationship. The past may have been sad, but the future does not have to be. If you don't like who you have been, you can be someone you would like a lot better. Love and romance are not for the young alone, they are also for the midlife person. So you're not perfect; nobody else is either. You don't have to be perfect. You still have a lot to offer someone. Concentrate not on what you don't have to offer, but on what you do.

Another reason starting over at midlife can be so scary is because it means starting to date people all over again, something most have not done since the late teens or early twenties. Many things have changed since then. Women may now take the initiative in asking a man for coffee, lunch, or dinner. Women are permitted to pick up the check some of the time. And the worrisome question is not how long before we kiss, but how long before we have sex. One man told me that a single woman acquaintance of his, showed up at his apartment door one night, and informed him that she thought he might be lonely and lacking a decent meal since his separation from his wife. So she had picked out some steaks, a bottle of wine and threw a nightgown in with the groceries. Not having dated anyone since the late fifties, he was dumbfounded.

There is a positive side to starting over—it can make you feel young again. So what if you feel a little bit sensitive and unsure of yourself. You have had years of experience. You have gained a lot of wisdom you never had when you were eighteen. You can do a better job of dating because you are wiser. You can now recognize a "line" a mile away. Besides, chances are your dating partner is feeling about as awkward as you are.

Almost every time I speak to a group about starting over at midlife, someone asks me where one can go to meet people of the opposite sex when you are over the age of forty. My questioners usually add quickly that they do not want to meet women or men in bars. My first answer is, that there are nice people who go to bars for a cocktail after work or before dinner, but I also know that there are places with the reputation of being "meat shops," and that a lot of people rightly feel humiliated going to a place like that.

The real answer to the question of where to go to meet people varies widely, depending on the kind of community you live in. In rural areas, this can be especially difficult; but there are rural churches that band together to provide a place for divorced and widowed people to get together. A rural client of mine tells me she is involved with a "single farmers" group that includes men and women. Another client became the driving force in getting a group of midlife singles going in her area.

In large metropolitan areas, there are usually many groups. Some of these are focused on divorce recovery, some on widow and widower experiences, and some on recreational activity alone. We now have both national and regional agencies that provide assistance in meeting other people. I have had some clients who speak highly of the people they have met by utilizing one of these services, but others have been disappointed. So much depends on how honestly people represent themselves. I always advise caution and suggest that people read the fine print. I certainly do not think that people should expose some very personal and private things about themselves that may find their way into somebody's database. Most of these people-meeting-people services do not ask for much more than superficial information to match people with similar interests and to rule out smoking, wide age differences, and clashing life styles.

I would have the same comments about the people-seeking-people ads in the daily newspapers. I once had the occasion to read one of the ads composed by a client, and, I must say, she widely misrepresented herself. Not everybody does, but again caution is the word. The same goes for meeting through electronic mail or in an internet chatroom. There has been national attention focused on the abuses of this kind of connection, including cases of older men meeting underage females, but any system is only as good as the honesty and integrity of those who are using it. Some methods are, however, more susceptible to abuse than others.

Many people meet other people through mutual friends, and I do not think there is anything wrong in asking your friends to keep an eye out for you. What you need to work at is being involved in activities that give you the opportunity to meet people. Activities that come to mind include serving on the board of directors of a United Way-supported agency, volunteering for special events in the community such as the Special Olympics, joining a book discussion group, or becoming a member of a fitness center. Coffee bars are also becoming popular places to meet others. The idea is to place yourself as often as you can where there are numbers of people. When you do, you raise the odds that you will meet someone.

I don't mean to suggest that everyone should be working on getting remarried. Absolutely not. It depends on whether that's what you want or not. If you want to get remarried, that's fine. I will talk about remarriage at midlife in the next chapter. But you may have a very full life without remarriage. Some people get very involved with grandchildren. Some have close relationships with others, even intimate and fully satisfying relationships without wanting to get remarried. Forced marriages at any age are not a good idea.

Life is intended to be lived and lived fully. We only get one life in this world, and even though we are living longer, it is still too short to live it in misery. That is not necessary. We read about the lives of people all the time who face crippling limitations to their lives, but who manage to rise above them and find meaning, purpose, and happiness.

Chapter Eight
Remarriage at Midlife

NEW RELATIONSHIPS AT MIDLIFE

There are, to be sure, many people who decide to remarry after divorce or the death of a spouse. Remarriages are being contracted at the rate of thirteen hundred a day in America. I am using the term *remarriage* to refer to a marriage in which one or both spouses has been married before. At the present time, slightly over half of the marriages contracted each year in America are remarriages instead of first marriages. Almost three fourths of the men who divorce will remarry, and approximately two thirds of the women who divorce will. While these numbers indicate more men than women will remarry research also shows that the older and more highly educated a woman is, the less likely that she will remarry. Morbidity statistics reveal that the pool of available men shrinks faster because men do not live as long as women, but there is an even more significant obstacle for women. Not only does the pool of eligible men shrink, but the men in that pool are capable of attracting and marrying younger women. While the age difference between men and women in first marriages is usually two to four years, in remarriages the age difference is more likely to be six to ten years. The older woman is thus competing against younger women for the same pool of males. In a culture that worships youth but still wants husbands to be older than wives, the outcome of that competition is predictable.

What about the prospect for remarriages being successful? Unfortunately, the divorce rate for remarriages is about ten percent higher than it is for first marriages, which is a real tragedy. People supposedly leave their first marriage because of deep unhappiness and with the conviction that a much better relationship than the one they are living is possible. They then enter a second marriage, only to find that this one is not only not happier, but may be worse.

Why is there such a problem with remarriage? The first reason why remarriages have problems is because we conceptualize them in the same way we conceptualize first marriages. A remarriage is not just another marriage; but especially when there are children involved, even adult children. We have all sorts of models and paradigms for first marriages, but in our culture we have none for remarriage. As a result, many people make plans for and think of their remarriage as though it is very much like going into a first marriage. I frequently speak to groups of clergy on marital and family issues and take the opportunity to ask them about what they do in premarital counseling with people who are remarrying. Most of them tell me they put them through the same material as first-time people. This will simply not work.

Another reason why some people in remarriages have such major problems is because, for one or both of the parties involved, there has not been a real emotional divorce from the previous marriage. In the previous chapter, I explained that the last step in the divorcing process was the "letting go." There is no emotional separation until then. Many people suppose that the emotional divorce and the legal divorce happen at the same time, but that is not true. For some, the emotional divorce actually precedes the legal divorce; for others, it comes long after. Many people do not understand that anger, bitterness, and resentment connect us emotionally to people just as powerfully as love does. Therefore, the presence of intense anger toward an ex-spouse is a sign that one is still not emotionally free of the former relationship. One must let go of that before trying to establish a relationship with someone else.

Wayne and Gloria met each other in a divorce recovery group. Both were divorced because their respective spouses left them for someone else. Wayne's spouse left him for a man that she worked with; Gloria's spouse left her after a two year involvement with one of her friends. Wayne and Gloria decided that they had a lot in common and spent a great deal of their time telling each other horror stories from their former marriages. Just six months after they met, they got married. I saw them about six months into their marriage. They indicated that during the first six months of their married life, they were involved mostly in trying to make life miserable for their ex-spouses. Wayne had been trying to jeopardize the job of the man with whom his wife had been involved and to whom she was now married. He was also trying to terminate the custody arrangement of the children so that he and Gloria could have them. Gloria was doing her best to make life miserable for her ex-spouse by frustrating his efforts to spend time with their children. Now, Wayne and Gloria were beginning to snap at each other. Their plots against ex-spouses were running up legal bills, and they were beginning to discover that there were basic characteristics about each other that they did not like. Sadly, what they had most in common with each other was their bitterness toward ex-spouses. The marriage did not celebrate the first anniversary.

Remarriages that began as affairs during the previous marriage do not do well either. In fact, it is one of the predictors of a troubled remarriage. It must be realized that an affair is not a marriage, and that there is much about the conduct of both people in an affair that gives a false sense of compatibility to the relationship. First, it is surrounded by secrecy, which means it is not lived in the real world. You have no idea what a relationship is really like until it can be lived out in the open. The effort that both people make to keep it a secret looks like an investment in the relationship but it isn't; it is merely an investment in self-protection. Secondly, because time together is so limited, and therefore precious, there is a false sense of the quality of intimacy in the relationship. You don't want to say or do anything that will spoil the time together, but true intimacy must be open, free, and lived with integrity. What does happen sometimes is that a relationship that begins as an affair in a former marriage does not make it to remarriage. When one or both people get out of an unhappy relationship, they experience such a sense of freedom that they have second thoughts about giving it up. The point I want to underscore is that the intensity of an affair is no sure sign of a quality relationship. It is really separateness masquerading as intimacy.

THE PROBLEMS OF NEW RELATIONSHIPS

Most of the problems associated with remarriage at midlife, or at any other time, have to do with the many ways in which remarriage is an altogether different genre of marriage than a first marriage. Let me explain briefly some of the differences.

The People Involved

In a first marriage, the people involved are the bride with her family and the groom with his family. The normal pattern is for both of them to move out of the parental home physically, if they haven't already, and to establish a living place of their own together. In a remarriage, there is a bride, a groom, the parents of each, the children of each from the previous marriages (even if they are adults), and the previous spouses of each, who have an abiding interest in the shared responsibility of parenting their children. Instead of being able to establish a tight boundary around their marital unit, the situation demands a very permeable boundary so that lots of people can move in and out. The remarried bride typically has the primary care and custody of her children from the first marriage, and the remarried groom has visitation rights with his children from his former marriage. With far more people involved, life is going to be much more complicated.

Emotional Ties

In a first marriage neither the bride nor the groom has any emotional ties to someone that predate the wedding, except to their own family of origin. In a remarried family, each will have emotional ties to their children. Those ties are stronger, and in the emotional dynamics of the remarried couple, each will feel, at times, that their spouse is putting the relationship with his or her children ahead of the marital relationship. This issue is still present when the children are older and have moved out of the home. When children need help, they go back to their parents, so stress can occur even with adult children. In addition, there is an ex-spouse with whom there was an emotional connection, even if it is now completely broken. Ex-wives and ex-husbands can be far more troublesome and threatening than ex-girlfriends and ex-boyfriends, because they have some excuse to interfere in the interests of children to which they are still emotionally connected.

The Order of Adjustment

In the typical first marriage, the couple has a chance to get adjusted to each other before they have to begin adjusting to children. In a remarried family the couple must adjust to each other and to all the children involved at the same time. In addition, some of the children may not be interested in bonding with their new stepparent. There are many factors that influence the time it takes for emotional bonds to develop between stepparents and stepchildren, but it will take years, not months.

Stepparenting

Here the problems are numerous. In many midlife marriages, there are still children in the remarried family. The children have lived part of their lives in the parenting pattern that developed between their biological parents. Now they come together in a stepfamily in which the former pattern will be different because the mix between biological parent and nonbiological parent will not be the same. To make matters even more complicated, children will often move back and forth from one remarried family to another, and in neither case will life be like it used to be. Think of all the things that are affected: discipline, eating habits, chores around the home, dress habits, expected manners, household rules, and tolerance of various behaviors. There are lots of places here for severe conflict to erupt.

Assessment of Happiness

Perhaps most significant of all is the criteria used by the marital couple to assess their marital happiness or the quality of the marriage relationship. In a first marriage, the couple makes that assessment on the basis of the dynamics between the two of them. How they treat each other and feel with each other is what counts. That is not the case in a remarried family. In that situation people judge the quality of their marriage on the basis of their relationship with each other's children. I have heard many remarried couples, on the brink of separation, affirm that when it is just the two of them, everything is fine; but when they must deal with the children, it is unbearably stressful.

DEALING WITH PROBLEMS

Hal and Linda's remarriage is troubled by the issues I have just described. They have been married for eighteen months; both were previously married. Hal was married to Becky for ten years, and together they had three children; the oldest and youngest are girls, the middle child is a boy. Linda was married previously to Chuck for eight years and has two boys. Hal has made no attempt to get very emotionally involved with either of Linda's two boys. Throughout their eighteen-month courtship and the eighteen months of married life, Hal and Linda have been embroiled in constant conflict. Linda indicates that her irritation is that Hal's first wife, Becky, is irresponsible as a mother and a spoiled brat as a person. Linda believes that Becky takes advantage of Hal by calling him and asking him if he will take the kids at other times than his scheduled visitation times, which is very disruptive to her plans. Also, Becky is frequently not home when Linda and Hal bring the children back after they have had them for the weekend, and she frequently wants to shuffle the visitation weekends. Linda is an organizer who goes to great trouble to see that on the weekends Hal does not have his children, she will also not have hers because they will be with their father. Her planning gets all messed up when Becky wants to make exchanges. Hal, on the other hand, feels badly about not getting to spend more time with his children. He insists he is not being used at all, but willingly agrees to have his children at other times than the visitation. Linda believes that Hal puts his relationship with his children ahead of their marriage relationship. Hal believes that Linda is forcing him to choose between her and his children. Hal would really like to get the primary care and custody of his children, because he does not think that Becky is a competent mother.

Linda, in other words, is trying to draw some fairly strong boundary around herself and Hal, but Becky is a powerful influence in their home. This outside influence is an issue that first marriages deal with only when the influence is the parents of one of the two. In the case of a parent, one can presume a good intention at least, and the problem can usually be dealt with as long as the child of that parent is willing to be firm. In this case, no such presumption of good intentions can be made. I had no idea whether Becky was aware of how much upset it caused in Hal's marriage when she wanted to shift weekends. I certainly suspect that she may be a fairly irresponsible parent since she is chronically late getting home on nights the children are being returned. My guess is that she is late for lots of things.

So how do we help Hal and Linda? They have lots of control over their own behavior and significant influence over their children's behavior, but none at all over Becky's. My suggestion is that they together agree on the limits they will set as far as Becky wanting to change arrangements. Since she is the one who wants more flexibility, she needs to be told that there can be greater flexibility only if she becomes more responsible about being home when the children are supposed to be dropped off. In this particular case, I also suggested to Hal that he become more involved with Linda's children which would, I thought, make her a lot more willing to have his children there at times other than scheduled visitations. I also suggested that, when they agree on a strategy, they need to stick to it. In addition, I suggested that Hal tell Becky he would no longer discuss arrangements concerning the children when she called him at work. She will have to call Hal at home, so that he can immediately talk the request over with Linda and they can together agree on a strategy.

Chad and Sherrie have a different problem. They have been married for two years and have a new baby boy, three months old. Both have been married before; Chad is ten years older than Sherrie. Chad left his former wife when she developed a mental illness that made it impossible for him and his children. He has custody of his four children from that marriage, ranging in age from eighteen to ten. Sherrie has one child by a previous marriage, a boy twelve. The boy lives with Sherrie's parents because of some special schooling he can get there. Chad is extremely disappointed with Sherrie because he believes that she has made no attempt to have a close relationship with his four children. Chad married Sherrie because he believed that she had the kind of qualities that would make her a good mother, but his children seem to prefer to spend lots of time in their own rooms and Sherrie does little to reach out to them. They had a courtship of only a few months, and Sherrie got pregnant very early in the marriage. Chad believes that since his children did not get much healthy attention from their mother, it is important for Sherrie to do a better job of building a close emotional bond with them.

This is a problem of unrealistic expectations that one finds very often with remarried families. Chad believed that, by two years into the marriage, things should be a lot cozier between Sherrie and the children, but the truth is that it takes much more time than that for a remarried family to come together and feel and act like family. Most experts believe that it takes at least three to five years for family formation to take place, and that when you factor in any teenagers, you will probably have to double that. This is because a primary developmental task of a teen is to learn to leave the family, and this is at odds with the developmental task of the new marriage, which is to become more cohesive. Chad had three teenagers plus a brand new baby, and yet he expected family formation to be almost complete. It is true that when a remarried couple has a baby of its own, it seems to speed up the remarried family formation, but in this case there are still those teenagers, plus the fact that Sherrie's own son is not with them.

I can still remember the movement of my own remarried family toward formation. There was a Christmas dinner with everybody together that was a delight. I remarked to my wife that it was the first time that it seemed like we were a real family. She shared the same feeling. We had started with four teenagers. Just four weeks before that Christmas dinner, we had celebrated our ninth wedding anniversary. Remarriage takes patience.

One of the big problems that may develop with remarriage at midlife is that one spouse, typically the man because he gets remarried to a younger woman, ends up with stepchildren significantly younger than his own. This means that he will have to go through some of the stages of child development with his stepchildren that he has already been through with his own children. Some men may discover that they resent that; others may discover that some of the issues that became conflicted when their own children went through that stage repeat themselves with their stepchildren. The problem is that, with your own children, when the times get really rough it helps that you can remember the good times in the past. This daughter who is so hard to control now was so cute and lovable when she was six, and so on. With stepchildren there are no pleasant times to recall that can sustain you through the bad times.

While this is not a book about stepparenting, I believe that stepparents should not try to discipline their stepchildren until some emotional bonding takes place. That may be never, or it may be several years down the line. Biological parents should discipline their own children. I know there will be times when, because you are the only one who is on the scene you may have to do it, but I believe that even then you say, "I believe your mother would say no to this kind of request, so that's what I'm going to say." Or, "you know what your mother has told you about that." In other words, you are just the voice of the other parent.

Remarriage at midlife must take into consideration that the life-cycle tasks of any adolescents involved are at cross purposes with the major task of the remarried family. It is an appropriate developmental task for adolescents to begin to pull away from their nuclear family, and they do this at a time when the developmental task of the remarried family is to pull together. While the family is attempting to build cohesiveness, the adolescent is building independence from the family. This is undoubtedly why remarried family formation must take longer when it involves at least one adolescent. Couples who are getting remarried at midlife will often be involved with adolescents, so this too puts a special strain on midlife remarried persons.

The stepchild/stepparent relationship, in other words, is so crucial to the perceived happiness and quality of a remarriage that it cannot be treated as one of several important issues. It is *the central issue* for remarriage. It is not enough for the remarried couple to succeed as husband and wife; they must also succeed as parent figures to each other's children. Howard is a divorced professional pilot who has been dating Marie for about a year. Marie is also divorced and came out of a verbally and physically abusive relationship. When Howard and Marie are together by themselves they have what each describes as an ideal relationship. Marie has two sons who live with her, however, and neither of the sons cares to have a relationship with his biological father who is remarried with young children. Marie's two sons, one eighteen and the other sixteen, are both doing poorly in school. The oldest dropped out of college before the end of the first semester; the youngest is making very poor grades in high school. She knows that both boys are using marijuana. She endures severe verbal abuse from them, and they frequently treat her with the same kind of contempt she experienced with their father. They usually do not do this when Howard is around, but he is aware of it and can barely contain his dislike for these two boys. When Howard is around, he refuses to get into a casual conversation with them and does his best to ignore them. The boys, quite obviously, experience Howard's dislike, which is not terribly different from what they experience with their father. As much as Howard and Marie want to get married, Howard is not willing to go ahead until both of the boys are gone. He appears to believe that, once the boys are gone, he will not have to deal with them and they will not be able to interfere in the marriage between him and their mother. Howard is wrong. The boys are not going to go away. In fact, it appears they are both having trouble with their own developmental tasks, which should take them to emotional maturity and economic independence. They are likely to be dependent upon their mother and Howard for quite a while.

The situation of Howard and Marie and Marie's two sons illustrates two realities about remarried families. The first reality is that when children do not have a good relationship with one of their biological parents, they have trouble developing a good relationship with a stepparent of the same gender. You might think this would not be the case, especially in a situation where two boys are experiencing what can only be called abandonment by their father. But even in the case of abandonment, the principle holds true that the relationship with a stepparent mirrors the relationship with the same gender biological parent. Ordinarily, it does not work for someone like Howard to butt in on this kind of situation. In this case, however, I urged Howard to get more involved. Howard's own children are older and on their own. He had some problems with one of his children, a daughter, around his divorce from her mother. He does not like confrontation and it is hard for him to do it, especially with someone's else's child. Since he is not yet married to their mother, it also limits what he can appropriately say, but I think he can and must say more if he wants eventually to marry Marie. I think he has to say to these boys, "Listen fellows, I am interested in having a more comfortable relationship with you. I can't be your Dad, but I can be closer to you than I am now and I would like to be. But I cannot do that as long as you treat your mother the way you do. When you are ready to clean up your act and be more civil and polite to your mother, I am ready to work at a better relationship between us. What do you think?" He could go one more step and say, "I don't have the right to say anything more to you right now. She is your mother. But when we get married, she will be my wife; and I will tell you right now that I will not allow you to treat my wife that way."

Howard does need to recognize that these boys are dealing with the primary rejection that they experience in relation to their father, and that his rejection of them, even though he is angry for a good reason, only reinforces their pain. By telling them that he would like to have a better relationship with them, he is letting them know that he, too, notices that it is not good now but that he is willing to work on it to make it better. That's more than their father seems willing to do.

The other reality about remarried families that Howard is not facing is that Marie will assess her marriage to him on the basis of his relationship with her children. Right now she feels caught between her children and Howard. She does not like the abuse she gets from them, and clearly she has not helped the situation by tolerating it for so long; but she also feels sorry for her sons because of the rejection they feel from their biological father. If this does not change, eventually she will resent Howard for his treatment of her sons, and that will hurt their marriage.

Because dealing with stepchildren in a midlife remarriage is so important, I have given a lot of thought to the problem of the lack of a clear paradigm for what it means to be a stepparent. Most of the notions of stepparent and step-child in our culture are negative. There is something pejorative about being a stepchild, or a stepmother. Stepchildren are sort of like orphans. The adjective that goes with stepmother is "wicked," and the incidence of sexual abuse by stepfathers is also well known.

I have been searching for some time for some model in our culture that I could point people to and say, "See, that's what its like to be a stepparent." The best one that I can come up with is to note the role of the understudy in a Broadway musical. The understudy is the backup in the event that the star is unable to perform. He or she must know all the lines, all the cues, all the dance steps, but must be content to have an anonymous place in the chorus line. The understudy does not get to be the star, but the moment will come, probably, when the star is unable to perform. Then the director says, "You're on!" The understudy will have a place in the sun for a few hours, but when the star returns, it's back to the chorus line, back to being anonymous. That is what it is like to be a stepparent. Your stepchild is the director, and you need to know everything that is going on in the life of the child; you have to know all the moves and all the right lines and all the cues. When your stepchild comes to you, it's the director saying, "You're on!" For a few moments you get to be on stage, and you dare not muff your lines. But make no mistake, you don't get to be the star. The best that can happen is that, after several years, you get to be a star in your own right; but you never get top billing.

It takes a long time, but it is worth it. The relationship you build with your spouse's children will give an extra bit of satisfaction to the marriage relationship like nothing else I know. Down the line, the reward for your effort is not that you get to be like a parent. That won't happen, no matter what. What you get to be is a trusted and valued friend.

RELATIONSHIPS WITHOUT CHILDREN

Couples in midlife relationships in which there are no children, or in which the children are adults living on their own, will not face problems with the severity of those described involving stepchildren, there are still other issues that must be acknowledged. Midlife relationships that do not involve children living at home have a much easier time simply because there is less tension. The basic "I" to "We" adjustment still exists, but most people at midlife are mature enough and have enough experience with relationships in general, that they make that adjustment much more easily than younger people do.

What requires the most attention in midlife relationships without children is the financial issue. The couple needs to discuss and resolve things such as what will happen with assets that were accumulated before the couple came together. Are there financial obligations to aging parents or to adult children to which one is committed? Who will pay for what in the new relationship? Financial advisors or tax attorneys are more helpful with these financial issues than are most counselors. Resolutions of these issues are sometimes dealt with quite formally by signing agreements, and I recommend this approach.

Finally, it is important to emphasize that many people do a much better job of working at relationships in midlife than they did earlier; and many of the relationships that are established at midlife are extremely happy and fulfilling. I believe that if counselors, psychologists, and ministers would do a better job of preparing people for midlife relationships, the success rate would be even higher.

Epilogue

I hope this book reflects a very positive outlook on love, on relationships, on marriage, and, with all of its challenges, on remarriage. The window through which I have looked and learned is the window between me and my clients. I have been looking through that window for forty years now, and, I hope, helping people to face the challenges of overcoming pain and having the courage to reach out again for love.

Life is a challenge. Love is a challenge. Marriage is a challenge. Parenthood is a challenge. But meeting challenges head-on is the way human beings grow. Midlife is also a time of challenge. As Erik Erickson understands it, we deal with the challenge of generativity and the anxiety of stagnation. Within our popular culture, midlife is still thought of mostly as a time of decline and diminishment. Perfect eyesight gives way to bifocals; the battle of the waistline gets more difficult; the job begins to be a bit of a drudge.

If the Jungians are correct, however, and I believe they are, life is not in some steep decline after age forty. Bifocals make it possible to see both the distant and the closeup things in life. All the parts of me that have been held back by my anxiety fight for their day in the sun. There is a whole other life to live, and a whole new half to life that is beginning. Forty is not the end of the good times. There is an anonymous saying that goes: Forty is the old age of youth; fifty is the youth of old age. So as I write at sixty-five, I insist I am only in the adolescence of old age. And that goes for you too. We really do have a chance to recreate ourselves at midlife. We have the chance to be the persons we have always wanted to be. We can conquer all the parts of us that have stood in the way of our growth and development as human beings. We can expand the parts of ourselves that have had little nourishment in the first half of life.

And we can love and be loved as never before. Stagnant relationships can become fresh again. Dead relationships can be resurrected. An old and tired marriage can be invigorated with new life. If necessary, new relationships can be created. The troubled waters of remarriage and stepfamilies can be safely negotiated with concerted effort and a lot of patience.

Midlife, in other words, need not be seen or experienced as a time of beginning decline. It is really a beginning, the beginning of the second half of your life; and love belongs as much in the second half of life as it does in the beginning. Saint Paul, in his beautiful hymn about love in the thirteenth chapter of 1 Corinthians, says that of all the gifts that humans may know, the greatest of all is love; and that any gift, sacrifice, or greatness that is not accompanied by love is of no value. As important as faith and hope are, they will come to an end; but not love. Love endures forever. Love outlasts everything. So give generously the love you have to offer your beloved and treasure the love you receive in return.

Suggested Reading

Bergquist, William H., Elinor Miller Greenberg, and G. Alan Klaum. *In Our Fifties: Voices of Men and Women Reinventing Their Lives.* San Francisco: Jossey-Bass, 1993.

Bradshaw, John. *Homecoming.* New York: Bantam, 1990.

Brewi, Janice, and Anne Brennan. *Celebrate Midlife: Jungian Archetypes and Midlife Spirituality.* New York: Crossroad, 1988.

————. *Midlife: Psychological and Spiritual Perspectives.* New York: Crossroad, 1991.

Carter, Betty, and Monica McGoldrick. *The Changing Family Life Cycle: A Framework for Family Therapy.* 2d ed. New York: Gardner Press, 1988.

Countryman, William. *Dirt, Greed and Sex: Sexual Ethics in the New Testament and Their Implications for Today.* Philadelphia: Fortress, 1988.

Faucett, Robert, and Carol Ann Faucett. *Intimacy and Midlife: Understanding Your Journey with Yourself, Others and God.* New York: Crossroad, 1990.

Fromm, Erich. *The Art of Loving.* New York: Harper and Row, 1956.

Friedman, Edwin. *Generation to Generation: Family Process in Church and Synagogue.* New York: Guilford Press, 1985.

Gerzon, Mark. *Listening to Midlife: Turning Your Crisis into a Quest.* Boston: Shambala, 1996.

Hardin, Paula Payne. *What Are You Doing with the Rest of Your Life?: Choices in Midlife.* San Rafael: New World Library, 1992.

Hendrix, Harville. *Getting the Love You Want.* New York: Henry Holt, 1988.

Hochschild, Arlie. *The Second Shift: Working Parents and the Revolution at Home.* New York: Viking, 1989.

Levinson, Daniel J., with Charlotte Darrow, Edward B. Klein, Maria H. Levinson, and Braxton McKee. *The Seasons of a Man's Life.* New York: Ballantine Books, 1978.

Lewis, Jerry, M.D. *The Birth of the Family: An Empirical Inquiry.* New York: Brunner/Mazel 1989.

Osherson, Sam. *Finding our Fathers: The Unfinished Business of Manhood.* New York: Free Press, 1986.

Pasley, Kay, and Marilyn Ihinger-Tallman, eds. *Remarriage and Stepparenting: Current Research and Theory.* New York: Guilford Press, 1987.

Sager, Clifford J. *Treating the Remarried Family.* New York: Brunner/Mazel, 1983.

Stein, Murray. *In Midlife: A Jungian Perspective.* Dallas: Spring Publications, 1983

Vaughan, Diane. *Uncoupling: Turning Points in Intimate Relationships.* New York: Vintage Books, 1987.

Visher, E. B. and J. Visher. *Old Loyalties, New Ties: Therapeutic Srategies with Stepfamilies.* New York: Brunner/Mazel, 1987.

Wallerstein, J. and J. B. Kelly. *Surviving the Breakup: How Children and Parents Cope with Divorce.* New York: Basic Books, 1979.

Index